The Natural Resource Content
of United States Foreign Trade
1870–1955

The Natural Resource Content
of United States Foreign Trade
1870–1955

by Jaroslav Vanek

The M.I.T. Press, *Cambridge, Massachusetts, 1963*

To Charles P. Kindleberger

Preface

To JAROSLAV VANEK falls the distinction of being the first contributor to a new series of published dissertations by recipients of the Ph.D. in economics at M.I.T. This series will consist of dissertations whose preparation, revision, and publication are supported by a grant to the Department of Economics from the Ford Foundation for that purpose. On behalf of the Department and the present and prospective authors, I should like to express our gratitude to the Foundation for making this project possible.

From its small beginnings just before World War II, our Ph.D. program in economics has achieved, we feel, some considerable measure of excellence. One indication of that accomplishment lies in the Ph.D. dissertations already published on an individual basis. These are:

1. Lawrence Robert Klein — *The Keynesian Revolution.* New York, The Macmillan Co., 1947.

2. George Pratt Shultz — *Pressures on Wage Decisions: A Case Study in the Shoe Industry.* Cambridge and New York, The Technology Press of The Massachusetts Institute of Technology and John Wiley & Sons, 1951.

3. George Benedict Baldwin — *Beyond Nationalization: The Labor Problems of British Coal.* Cambridge, Harvard University Press, 1955.

4. Leslie Cookenboo, Jr. — *Crude Oil Pipe Lines and Competition in the Oil Industry.* Cambridge, Harvard University Press, 1955.

5. Louis Lefeber — *Allocation in Space, Production, Transport and Industrial Location.* Amsterdam, North-Holland Publishing Company, 1958.

6. Bedros Peter Pashigian   *The Distribution of Automobiles: An Economic Analysis of the Franchise System.* Englewood Cliffs, N.J., Prentice-Hall, 1961.

7. Egon Sohmen   *The Economics of Flexible Exchanges.* Chicago, University of Chicago Press, 1961.

8. John Lawrence Enos   *Petroleum Progress and Profits: A History of Process Innovation.* Cambridge, The M.I.T. Press, 1962.

Gratifying as this list is, it is our hope that it will be expanded at an accelerated rate under the new arrangement whereby more systematic aid and encouragement are available for the most promising of our Ph.D. dissertations. Support is needed in particular, we feel, for thesis projects whose scope or depth is appreciably greater than the average. We also hope that the goal of publication will become a more vivid one in the minds of all of our Ph.D. aspirants.

Professor Vanek's thesis research was initially supported by a fellowship grant from Resources for the Future, Inc., which has also made a contribution to the cost of the present publication. This help is gratefully acknowledged by all concerned.

ROBERT L. BISHOP
Head, Department of Economics and Social Science
Massachusetts Institute of Technology

Acknowledgment

THIS STUDY is the result of research undertaken for my doctoral dissertation presented at M.I.T. in 1957, and of a number of subsequent revisions. Important parts of the analysis that were included in my thesis have been taken out, and others added.

I am greatly obliged to Resources for the Future, Inc., for material support of my research in its various stages. I have also received much valuable advice and criticism from the members of that institution, and was permitted to use statistical material prepared in conjunction with other projects of the R.F.F. Among those of the organization who extended their helping hand Professor Harold Barnett deserves special thanks.

Professor Charles Kindleberger not only was the first to suggest the topic of this study but also provided me with invaluable counsel through the different stages of its preparation. I received much constructive advice from Professor Robert Solow as well.

A grant from the Department of Economics of Harvard University enabled me to obtain statistical and computational assistance. Most of Chapter 9 of this study appeared in 1959 in the *Review of Economics and Statistics*. I herewith express my thanks to the editors of the *Review* for permission to reprint passages of the article.

JAROSLAV VANEK

Contents

CONTENTS

List of Figures

LIST OF FIGURES

List of Tables

The Natural Resource Content
of United States Foreign Trade
1870–1955

1

Introduction

THE increasing awareness of the importance of natural resources for
our national well-being and economic growth has been demonstrated
by the number of studies devoted to the problem in the postwar years,
and by the increasing concern of private and official institutions. In
spite of the fact that our national economy depends on foreign sources
for a good share of its resource supplies, and in spite of the fact that this
dependence is growing continuously, the literature dealing with the
specific question of foreign trade in natural resources is scanty. The
purpose of this study is to fill — within the modest means of the writer —
such a gap.

The study will be historical, examining American foreign trade in
natural resources over a period of 85 years. It will not be a mere narra-
tive of past events; rather, we want to identify the different forces that
have determined the natural resource content of our foreign trade, and
study their intensity.

The reader who expects to be confronted with a detailed analysis of
American foreign trade in individual primary products may be somewhat disappointed. It is just the opposite approach that we have adopted
in this study—most of our analysis deals with large aggregates of commodities. One practical reason led to the aggregative approach: A
detailed investigation covering United States imports and exports over
a period of 85 years was not feasible. The *primary* objective, however,
that we have pursued in dealing with aggregates, rather than individual
commodities, is to suggest an alternative method of economic analysis
aiming at a *rapprochement* between the theory of international trade and
its application to empirical problems.

The classical doctrine of international economics has used extreme
simplifications of reality in demonstrating its theorems. Recently,
theorists have attempted to construct more comprehensive trade models

1

of the general equilibrium type, but they have most often found it difficult to go beyond a mere description of reality.

On the other hand, empirical economists frequently either have not been able to use the oversimplified theories of international trade, because reality was much more complex, or could not use the general equilibrium models, because their complexity hindered derivation of meaningful results. And thus we find the empirical literature in the field of international economics well supplied with tedious commodity studies which often make very little use of the theory of international trade.

We certainly do not want to underestimate the merits of either theoretical or empirical economics. But the gap between economic theory and practice in the field of international economics seems unnecessary, and if it cannot be eliminated entirely, it may at least be reduced.

"Terms of trade" is a concept derived from a simple two-commodity theoretical model and currently used in international trade discussions. But in the eyes of the empiricist it is an index which also aggregates unit values of a large number of commodities. Those who prefer a partial analysis might argue that such an aggregate index has very little practical significance. It is difficult to refute such a criticism completely, because a case could always be found where an improvement in the terms-of-trade index did not guarantee an impact on, say, national welfare that would immediately follow in a situation when only one commodity was traded. Yet, we customarily identify the simple theoretical model with the real world and draw conclusions concerning the latter using theorems derived from the former. In 99 out of 100 cases, we can be sure we are right. It seems that many fields in the social sciences could not survive if such incompletely justified inferences, or logical jumps, were not made.

Most of the empirical analysis presented in this book is open to similar criticism. We believe, however, that imperfections arising from aggregation are a very small price to pay for the interesting results obtainable in this way which would otherwise be out of our reach.

To be more specific, the gap between pure theory and empirical economics can be bridged if we use the simple and workable theoretical models together with aggregates of real economic magnitudes which, for the purpose of analysis, are handled as single variables. In addition, in order to make such an approach meaningful, it is always necessary to learn something about the likelihood and nature of the biases which may arise in the process of aggregation.

It is no less legitimate to deal with natural resources or *natural resource products* as aggregates than it is to deal with an index of the terms of trade reflecting unit-value variations of thousands of commodities. The only difference is that in the first case we speak of an aggregate of values (or possibly quantities), while in the second we deal with prices or unit values. The important shortcoming, namely, our ignorance of the dispersion (or, in more technical terms, of the standard deviation) of changes within the aggregate, is the same in both situations.

Following the general approach that we have defended in the preceding paragraphs, this study logically falls into two different parts: one theoretical, one empirical. In the next three chapters we shall discuss the most important theoretical concepts and tools of measurement used in our inquiry. Alternative possibilities of measuring the natural resource content and the meaning of such indexes are examined in Chapter 2. Owing both to statistical and conceptual difficulties, "economic rent" is rejected as a workable device. Instead, content of resource products in any given bill of goods, expressed either in constant or current prices, is adopted. In order to establish at least approximately the relation between the resource product content on the one hand and the "true" resource content of trade (or any other collection of products) on the other, we examine, under simple assumptions, the stability of the relation between our estimator and the statistic actually measured. Although it is impossible to design a precise test of goodness of fit, there is a strong a priori presumption that with changing economic parameters, such as technology, factor endowments, and demand conditions, resource product requirements of large aggregates, such as exports or imports, will vary in proportion to the actual resource content.

Chapter 3 constitutes the theoretical key to our analysis. Using a simple two-commodity model, it shows how the resource structure of a country's foreign trade may be affected by changes in factor endowments, technology, and demand conditions. In essence, it adapts the factor-proportions theory of trade to the comparative-static framework of the present study.

Further clarification and adaptation of existing theory is presented in Chapter 4. There the factor-proportions theory, usually stated in terms of a two-country, two-commodity model, is adjusted to more realistic conditions where three groups of productive factors are used in producing large numbers of commodities. Clearly, it is impossible to restate the theory with a degree of rigor equal to its traditional form. Nevertheless, an approximate restatement is obtained, namely: The relative endowments of a country engaging in foreign trade will be reflected in the relative factor requirements of its exports and imports. A

[3]

later chapter uses this conclusion in analyzing the resource endowments of the United States.

Chapters 5 through 9 are devoted to the empirical study of the resource content of American foreign trade between 1870 and 1955. In Chapter 5 we amass and discuss the relevant information in its crudest form — only the direct resource product components of trade are considered. An over-all trend for the entire period shows a declining resource content in our exports and an increase in the proportion of resource products imported. An important asymmetry between exports and imports, however, is apparent. While the trend is smooth and very pronounced over the entire period on the export side, imports of resource products reached a maximum in about 1920, and their share in total imports remained fairly stable thereafter. All these measurements are expressed in terms of current values. The trends of export and import unit values for the different commodity groups, however, indicate that relative prices had very little effect on these variations and consequently that quite similar trends would have been found if volumes rather than values had been considered. An analysis of price-quantity fluctuations over the 11 key periods considered indicates an impact of foreign supply and demand conditions on our trade in resource products stronger than that of domestic conditions.

In Chapter 6 we study the relative importance of foreign trade in the total resource requirements of the United States. On the whole, the above trends are reflected in these findings, although a good deal of variation between different natural resource sectors, both in the time trends and absolute levels, is apparent. With the exception of a rather unimportant group of nonmetallic, non-fuel minerals, United States apparent consumption has increased faster than domestic output of resource products. This trend is most pronounced in the case of metallic ores, fishing and wild-life products, and agricultural non-food primary products. Except for primary foods, where, on balance, we produce just about as much as we consume, this country is a net importer of all resource products. The consumption of metallic ores in this country is today almost twice as high as domestic output.

Chapter 7 summarizes a vast amount of data and computational effort, of others and of our own, concerning the direct and indirect resource product requirements of American foreign trade. The input-output method is used here in evaluating total and sectoral requirements of American exports and competitive imports. The reader is referred to the chapter itself for the analysis of results and a discussion of the computational method.

[4]

Chapter 8 uses the theoretical analysis of Chapter 3, the results of the preceding empirical chapters, and some additional data in an attempt to identify the important long-run forces which have influenced the structure of American foreign trade during the period considered. For the purposes of this analysis a line is drawn between mineral and replaceable resources. Productivity changes and changes in factor endowments and tastes in the United States and abroad are examined in relation to the two broad resource sectors and to manufactured products. In spite of a very rapid growth of productivity in the mineral industries in the United States, probably much more rapid than abroad, such resources on net balance have demonstrated the fastest-growing deficiency. The demand conditions for minerals and the nonrenewable character of such products seem to explain this trend. The ratio between renewable resource products exported and imported, on the other hand, has declined only slightly over the entire period. The effects of Engel's law, together with United States farm policies, were able to outweigh, in this case, the comparatively slow growth of farm productivity through most of the period.

Two important questions are dealt with in the last empirical chapter of the book. First we attempt to use available statistics in estimating the true resource requirements of American foreign trade in order to obtain an over-all index of the relative abundance of United States natural resources as compared with the rest of the world. The results of the input-output analysis of Chapter 7 are used to construct an estimator of the statistic for the period 1870–1955. The second task of the chapter is to test Professor Leontief's "scarce-factor paradox" in light of the results of this study in establishing the relation between American factor endowments and the structure of foreign trade in 1947. It appears from the analysis here presented not only that the "paradox" may be explained by the existence of a third factor, i.e., land resources, but also that this factor has great importance in determining the composition of our exports and imports.

We make no attempt here to project past trends into the future. However unfashionable this omission may be, we believe that the number and importance of the unknown factors involved are so great that any long-range forecast would be of little value. Nevertheless, it is impossible to deny that a certain persistence of trends is often observed over time. But we leave it to the reader to use the findings and the analysis of international trade presented in this study in drawing his own conclusions as to the future resource requirements of American foreign trade. Actually, he will often find it necessary to weigh the different factors entering his forecast according to its purpose.

2

Measuring Resource Requirements of Trade

In a study dealing with the natural resource content of trade, the first task is to design a measure or expression of such a content. The task is not an easy one. Indeed, a number of theoretical and practical problems have to be confronted before a workable and meaningful concept of "resource content" is obtained.

Our task falls within two broad categories, and will be accomplished using these two categories in this chapter. First, we shall examine what would be the ideal measure of resource requirements of trade if there were no limitations stemming from a lack of statistical information. Second, however, such limitations will have to be taken into account in order to obtain an operational index of resource requirements for international trade.

From the outset, it will be observed that an index of resource requirements must serve two different purposes. On the one hand, it has to permit comparisons between different aggregates at a given single point in time; on the other hand, since this study is historical, it has to permit comparisons between different periods. In other existing studies of a similar kind — for example, Professor Leontief's analysis of labor and capital requirements of United States foreign trade[1] — it is evident that the latter dimension was absent, because no time comparisons were made.

Fundamentally, two distinct concepts of resource content may be employed. First, we can measure the physical volume of natural resources necessary in producing a given collection of products, such as those entering exports or imports. This concept of resource content is usually encountered in literature dealing with other productive factors. As long as there is only a single type of homogeneous natural resource,

[1] W. Leontief, "Domestic Production and Foreign Trade," *Proceedings of the American Philosophical Society*, 97, No. 4 (September 1953), pp. 332–347.

as is often assumed in purely theoretical discussions, this measure is entirely physical and does not require any valuation whatsoever. Second, the question can be asked: What productive contribution did natural resources supply in producing a given bill of goods (such as exports or imports), given the relative scarcities of productive resources in the economy? This latter criterion leads to a measure of the value of productive services of land that has been used in producing a given total value of exports or imports.

If comparisons over time are sought, the value of productive resources of land corresponding to the second definition must be deflated by some appropriate general price index, in order to eliminate the effect of possible changes of the general price level imputable to purely monetary phenomena. Indeed, doubling the supply of money that would double the value of rent contained in total value of exports has nothing to do with, nor does it indicate, an increase of productive contribution of domestic land resources to such exports. Such a deflation can be avoided if the resource content is measured as a share of some other aggregate, such as total value of exports or of imports, rather than in absolute terms.

If more than one homogeneous type of natural resource is used in producing exports or imports, even the first measure requires some valuation. Indeed, iron mines and wheat-land used as productive resources in manufacturing automobiles and flour for exports are two entirely different types of natural resources and can be combined in a single expression of resource content of exports only by means of some appropriate weights or coefficients. Unit values of different types of natural resources are such economically meaningful coefficients. Thus, the volume of each particular natural resource has to be multiplied by its unit value, and these products then can be added to obtain a single measure of resource content, using our first definition. In comparing volumes of natural resources used over time, changing amounts of different types of land also have to be combined by using some constant value-coefficient or some other procedure customary in index-number construction.

Because, under competitive conditions, unit land values in each period will be at least approximately proportional to unit land rents, our two concepts of resource content will lead to the same answers with regard to comparisons in a single period of time. Such comparisons can be made between the resource content of exports and of imports, between that of exports and of total national output, between the resource content of a given portion of exports and another one, and so on.

[7]

For comparisons between resource contents at different periods in time, the two distinct measures can no longer be considered equivalent. Depending on the movements of unit rents and the general price level over time, the two proposed measures of resource content will yield different time comparisons. For example, assume that with unchanged product prices the physical resource content (our first definition) of exports rises 50% in a given period, but that rents double. The natural resource content as expressed by the value of productive services of land, for the same exports, would then increase by 200%.

If a satisfactory index of unit rent changes over time is available for a particular bill of goods studied, together with an index reflecting general movements of prices, results obtained for one definition of resource content can easily be reworked into results for the other definition. It will be useful to retain this observation for our subsequent empirical discussion, where for practical reasons approximations of the second measure of resource content are sought.

Specifically, it can be stated that with I_{ph} representing the index of changes in the physical input of natural resources, I_{val} the index of resource content based on our second definition, I_p the index reflecting general movements of prices, and I_r the index reflecting changes in unit rents of land, the following relation must prevail between I_{ph} and I_{val}:

$$(1/I_p)I_r I_{ph} = I_{val} \qquad (2.1)$$

As an application, it will be observed that with unchanged physical natural-resource content and unchanged land rents, the index of resource content based on the second definition will decline with rising prices, land and its services having become relatively less scarce and less expensive. On the other hand, if rents had risen *pari passu* with the general price level, resulting from a monetary inflation, the resource content based on the second definition would also have remained unchanged, as would that based on the first definition.

To sum up the foregoing discussion in practical terms, we can say the following: For comparisons within a given year, the reckoning of the rent content of a given value aggregate expresses, at least as an approximation, both the physical natural-resource requirements and the productive contribution of natural resources to the particular aggregate. When comparisons over time are sought, the value aggregate (such as rent contained in total value of exports) has to be deflated by an index of changes in the unit rent of land if we want to obtain a measure corresponding to our first definition, and by an index of the general level of prices if a measure based on the second definition is sought.

In practice, there are a number of difficulties hampering both approaches, some conceptual, some purely statistical. In the first place, there are almost no statistical data concerning rent of land, or detailed land-input coefficients. Second, even if competitive prices or rents of all types of land were recorded, we would still run into many difficulties of definition.

The few estimates of rent that one can find in the literature are too aggregative and crude to be useful. *Agricultural Statistics*[2] currently publishes a series, begun in 1910, that gives the net farm rent paid to non-farm landlords. Professor T. W. Schultz[3] estimates the contribution of land to total agricultural inputs for 1910–14 and for 1945–48, using work done by G. T. Barton and M. R. Cooper and that of the Bureau of Agricultural Economics.[4] Even if one were not tempted to question the validity and precision of these estimates, they could not be used, since no information exists concerning rent by type of crop. The strong monopolistic elements and vertical integration often encountered in this sector introduce further complications.

For the statistician, rent always means payment for the services of an unseparable bundle of productive factors — capital and land. In fact, if we examined variation in statistically recorded rent over a long period of time, we would most likely find ourselves measuring the changes in capital invested in land rather than those of economic rent. For example, Professor Schultz finds that in the United States the value of farm buildings relative to total value of real estate has increased from 18 to 33% over the past 40 years.[5]

Ever since the first settlement in this country, soil has been improved; that is, capital has been invested in it. Over a long period of time, fertilizers were applied to certain lands, and not to others. Development of transportation facilities produced important external economies both in farming and in mining production. Imputation of these economies to particular outputs is virtually impossible.

It is impossible to separate with any degree of precision capital improvements from original land in any given lot of farmland, and a definition of mining resources is equally difficult. A little reflection will convince the reader of the impossibility of conceiving of

2 U.S. Dept. of Agriculture, *Agricultural Statistics*, 1952, p. 698.
3 T. W. Schultz, *The Economic Organization of Agriculture* (New York, McGraw-Hill, 1953), pp. 137, 211, 213.
4 G. T. Barton and M. R. Cooper, "Relation of Agricultural Production to Inputs," *Review of Economics and Statistics*, May 1948, pp. 117–128; unpublished information from the Bureau of Agricultural Economics.
5 T. W. Schultz, *op. cit.*, p. 137.

a homogeneous nonrenewable natural resource measurable in physical units.

One possibility of estimating rents would be to evaluate the cost of labor, capital, and materials, and find the residual (as did Ricardo). A good deal of effort was devoted to this approach in the early stages of our work. United States census data and many income statements of leading resource industries were consulted for this purpose; in no case, however, did we find all the information on a single year necessary for such estimates. We believe that the imputations, guesswork, and extrapolations which would be required to complete the information available would have been a more serious source of error than that with which we must cope in our adopted measure of resource requirements. Moreover, such statistical work bearing on the entire period of reference and attaining a reasonable coverage would have been beyond the possibilities of the present study.

Finally, we must keep in mind the fact that we are dealing with the resource content of both American exports and imports; hence, we would also need information concerning the rent of land, land-input coefficients, and/or land values in foreign countries. The use of domestic data in estimating the resource content of supplementary imports per dollar (as Professor Leontief has done for capital and labor)[6] might be justified. But if we used this approach, we would be forced to evaluate the "true" resource requirements of commodities which are not produced in this country.

The foregoing discussion is regarded as sufficient to justify the rejection of either of the two theoretical concepts as a workable statistical foundation for our empirical investigation. The substitute we have chosen is the "value of resource products." We define as resource products all commodities whose productive process makes direct use of natural resources, and for which values of output are currently recorded. Thus, wheat grain is a resource product, while wheat flour is not, since it does not use land as a direct input. If wheat were produced separately from stalks, we would consider stalks a resource product.

In practice — and this is of paramount importance for our subsequent empirical work — our definition conforms to two currently accepted concepts of statistical classification:

1. United States foreign trade returns present data for the entire period 1870–1955, divided into five commodity classes: raw materials, crude foodstuffs, manufactured foodstuffs, semi-

[6] Leontief, *loc. cit.*

manufactures, and manufactured products. The first two groups, according to our definition, are essentially resource products.

2. Resources for the Future, Inc., uses the classification of the Bureau of Labor Statistics, which divides the American economy into 192 sectors of production and defines 21 of these as resource industries.[7]

If economic rent were used directly as a measure of the resource content of American foreign trade, we would evaluate all rent of land paid in producing all exported and imported goods. Our indirect indicator will measure the value of resource products (as we have defined them) in total exports and imports. It is clear that only if resource products were produced from land alone, and other commodities from other factors of production, would our indicator reflect exactly the "true" resource content of foreign trade. Since this is generally not the case, our indirect measure will be subject to a number of different sources of bias.

The fundamental fact that allows us to substitute "resource products" for "rent of land" is that the "true" resource content of resource products is on the average considerably higher than that of more highly fabricated commodities. Common sense suggests that the value added (profits and wages) to the original value of natural materials for a finished car will far exceed that of the iron ore. Evidence provided by an input-output calculation made by Resources for the Future, Inc., points in the same direction.[8]

Since the resource content of resource products is considerably greater than for non-resource products, changes in the content of resource products in exports or imports will be a reflection of similar changes in the resource content. Similarly, an aggregate of commodities containing a greater value of resource products, both directly and indirectly, as inputs in other products (in the sense of the input-output analysis), can be expected to contain a higher proportion of natural resources.

With respect to the second definition of resource content, it can be postulated that changes in the volume of an aggregate of resource products in total exports or imports will be roughly proportional to changes in the resource content. To substantiate this proposition, let us first consider a simple situation where a single product using natural resources as an input is exported. It is further assumed that the industry

[7] The numbers of the Bureau of Labor Statistics classification corresponding to these industries are 1 through 20 and 36. See Table 7.2 in the appendix to Chapter 7.
[8] See the appendix to Chapter 7.

is competitive, and hence its technology can be described as one subject to constant returns to scale. Only one other factor of production is used.

For the resource content to be for each period proportional in this situation to the value of exports, the only requirements are: (1) that the elasticity of substitution of land for the other factor be unity, and (2) that technological change be neutral with respect to land and the other productive factor, that is, saving neither land nor the other factor. Under such conditions, changes in factor supplies, in technology, or in demand conditions that may change the volume and value of exports will leave unaffected the share of rent per dollar of exports.

In practice, any single product cannot be expected to have the desired properties of unit elasticity of substitution and neutral technological change. But, with a large number of resource products entering international trade, some products can have elasticities greater, and others smaller, than unity; some products may be subject to a land-saving innovation, others to a land-absorbing one. If such different properties of various products do not balance exactly in their effects, at least they can be expected to offset one another to a large degree and preserve approximately the postulated proportionality between the value of resource products traded and the value of land input of trade in a world of changing economic conditions.

Now if the current rent content and the value of exports or imports of resource products are approximately proportional at all times, changes in volumes of exports or imports of resource products ought to reflect approximately changes in the resource content on our second definition. Indeed, if the general price level had increased owing to monetary inflation, together with prices of resource products, such changes would be eliminated by using volumes rather than values. On the other hand, if the value of resource products traded had changed and no significant change of the general price level had taken place, such values could be expected to reflect the resource content of trade.

It is necessary to deflate values of resource products traded if we want to obtain an approximation of changing resource content in absolute terms. Such deflation, however, will not be necessary if we want to obtain an index of changes in the share of resource content in an aggregate value that is likely to involve price changes similar to those of the resource products. Thus the changes in time of the value of resource products measured as a share of total value of exports or imports can be expected to reflect changes of the true resource content relative to the total value of exports or imports.

An argument similar to that just expounded with regard to changing resource content over time can be extended, relying on the law of large numbers, to comparisons between different portions of exports or imports in a given year. Specifically, a sufficiently large aggregate of exports (such as that of primary foodstuffs) will contain approximately as many times more resource content than another (such as of manufactured products) as it contains more resource products than the other. Of course, we speak here of both direct and indirect resource product requirements.

Admittedly, the statistical method explained here and the inferences drawn are very crude ones, and later empirical analysis is accordingly approximate. Nevertheless, we believe that even in the absence of more accurate statistical information and greater resources than those available to the present writer, our empirical work is not without significance.

3

Long-Run Determinants of the Resource Structure
of International Trade

IN the preceding chapter we pointed out the difficulties arising in the actual evaluation of rent and attempted to justify the substitution of *resource products* for rent as a measure of resource content. The present chapter will deal with the theory underlying the changes in the commodity structure of foreign trade. It is on this commodity structure that the resource content of trade will depend.

The factor-proportions theory of international trade states that an economy will tend to export goods which use more intensively its most abundant factor of production.[1] Or, in terms of our analysis, we may state that the natural resource requirements of foreign trade will tend to reflect the relative abundance of natural resources in the economy. If, then, the relative abundance of natural resources is changing with time, it follows that,the natural resource content of international trade also changes, other things being equal, and so does the proportion of resource products in total exports or imports.

Hence, we want to introduce into our model the stock of natural resources as a changing parameter. Furthermore, in order to consider the factor intensity of production, the model must include its physical conditions (production functions). Finally, the conditions of demand will be examined. In other words, the opportunity cost curve will be used together with an indifference map,[2] and in addition, some resources (factors of production) will be allowed to vary in supply.

Let us first consider briefly an economy in isolation and ask how

---

[1] A rigorous statement of the theory requires certain precise qualifications concerning the nature of production functions, tastes, factor supplies, etc. These, however, are not essential to the present argument and will be discussed in more detail in the following chapter.

[2] A. P. Lerner, "The Diagrammatical Representation of Cost Conditions in International Trade," *Economica*, *12* (1932), pp. 346–356.

production and consumption are affected by changing resource endowments. The assumptions of our model are as follows:

Two goods, x_1 and x_2, are produced in a closed economy. Each is produced by two primary factors of production, v_1 and v_2. Hence, we can write the two production functions as

$$x_1 = x_1(v_1{}^1, v_2{}^1) \tag{3.1}$$

and

$$x_2 = x_2(v_1{}^2, v_2{}^2) \tag{3.2}$$

We further assume constant returns to scale; i.e., Equations 3.1 and 3.2 are linear homogeneous functions. Product x_1 is for any combination of factor prices more v_1-intensive than product x_2; that is,

$$\frac{v_1{}^1}{v_2{}^1} > \frac{v_1{}^2}{v_2{}^2} \quad \text{for any } \frac{\bar{v}_1}{\bar{v}_2} \qquad \checkmark$$

where barred variables stand for money wages.

Factor v_1 may be thought of as land (or natural resources) and v_2 as a composite dose of the remaining factors of production, say, labor and capital. Note that as long as we accept the unrealistic assumption that both prices and quantities of the two vary proportionally, this lumping together of two factors is legitimate for purposes of the analysis.

Each factor is perfectly inelastic in supply in the short run and v_1 (land) also in the long run. Factor v_2, on the other hand, is allowed to change over long periods of time (such as the five- or ten-year periods later considered in the empirical chapters). The total supply of v_2 at each period t, however, is predetermined independently of the economic circumstances of the period.[3] This, we admit, is a daring assumption for capital, if not for both factors entering v_2. Thus we have the following two relations:

$$v_1{}^1 + v_1{}^2 = v_1 \tag{3.3}$$

and

$$v_2{}^1 + v_2{}^2 = v_2(t) \tag{3.4}[4]$$

[3] Note that this assumption takes us out of the sphere of statics into that of comparative statics, not of dynamics. It would be easy to think of a dynamic model which would more closely reflect the conditions of the real world — e.g., by dating all our variables and making v_2 depend on past income, prices, stock of capital, etc. Such a model, however, would be completely nonoperational. Even our present model can be dealt with in a simple way only by geometrical methods. A mathematical analysis would be extremely laborious and possibly less illuminating.

[4] Note that perfectly inelastic supplies of productive factors are required for construction of a meaningful transformation function, i.e., one which satisfies the

One more equation is required to obtain the usual transformation function (opportunity cost curve) $T(x_1, x_2) = 0$,[5] which gives the maximum producible amount of one commodity when we are given the amount of the other commodity produced. This is given by the marginal conditions of production, namely,

$$\frac{\dfrac{\partial x_1}{\partial v_1{}^1}}{\dfrac{\partial x_1}{\partial v_2{}^1}} = \frac{\dfrac{\partial x_2}{\partial v_1{}^2}}{\dfrac{\partial x_2}{\partial v_2{}^2}} \tag{3.5}$$

We have thus a system of five equations in seven variables, namely, x_1, x_2, $v_1{}^1$, $v_1{}^2$, $v_2{}^1$, $v_2{}^2$, and $v_2(t)$. The last is the changing capital and labor factor of production. This system can be reduced to one equation in x_1, x_2, and the parameter $v_2(t)$:

$$T[x_1, x_2, v_2(t)] = 0 \tag{3.6}$$

Let us for the moment hold $v_2(t)$ fixed and examine the meaning and some of the characteristics of T. Each point of T gives the maximum of either product that the economy will produce for a given amount of the other product. All points bounded by T and the two axes are feasible, yet it is always in the interest of the society to move to the frontier T.[6] Any point not within this area cannot be attained by the productive capacity of the economy. From our assumptions of linear homogeneity of the production functions (i.e., constant costs of production) and uniformly greater land intensity of x_1 over x_2, it follows that T will be a

---

optimum marginal conditions. If factors are assumed to be variable with factor or goods prices, a locus expressing optimal productive capacity of the economy again is defined, but it generally does *not* satisfy the marginal conditions any more. In other words, the price ratio between x_1 and x_2 is no longer equal to the slope of this locus at the point at which the economy produces.

The variable supply of factors of production, besides complicating considerably the construction of a meaningful efficiency locus, endangers the validity of the Heckscher–Ohlin theorem. Under such conditions an economy *may* appear both relatively abundant or relatively poor in a given factor of production, depending on relative factor and goods prices.

[5] The derivation of T can be demonstrated by the Edgeworth box diagram. Although it is omitted here, reference is made to W. Stolper and P. A. Samuelson, "Protection and Real Wages," reprinted in the American Economic Asociation, *Readings in the Theory of International Trade* (Philadelphia, Blakiston, 1950), pp. 333–357.

[6] The assumption of fixed factor supplies implies that no disutility is attached to these factors of production.

monotonically decreasing function convex upward. One such typical contour is shown in Figure 3.1.

What will happen if we allow $v_2(t)$ to assume different values? Obviously, an increase of the capital-labor factor will expand the transformation contour. All the general characteristics described above will be preserved. But what can we say about the nature of the expansion, that is, about the relative increases of the production possibilities of x_1 and x_2? As both industries are users of both factors, an increased supply of v_2 will be shared by both. Hence, the increased productive capacity will go into both x_1 and x_2; in particular, both axis intercepts will move away from the origin. As to the relative shares of both industries from an increased stock of v_2, the (relatively) v_2-intensive product x_2 will be favored.

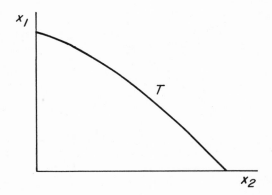

Figure 3.1. The production possibility curve.

This can be seen more clearly in Figure 3.2, where two box diagrams are superimposed on each other. The horizontal axis measures v_2, the vertical v_1. While the total supply of v_1 remains constant, two different total supplies of v_2 are allowed for, OB and OB', respectively. Our v_2-intensive commodity, x_2, is measured from O, the lower left-hand corner of the box, while x_1 is measured from the origins O' and O''. Let us recall, moreover, that both production functions are unit-homogeneous. We can visualize the process of the growth of one factor as a sliding of one isoquant plane (of x_1) on another fixed isoquant plane (of x_2). One contract curve (locus of tangency of isoquants of x_1 and x_2) such as OO' corresponds to each given level of v_2. Each contract curve corresponds to one transformation function (Equation 3.6); with

[17]

each point on the contract curve we can associate two numbers expressing the levels of isoquants of x_1 and x_2, tangential to each other at this point. By plotting these numbers in an $x_1 x_2$ plane, we obtain the transformation contour T (see Figure 3.1).

By going from O along the contract curve in the northeast direction, it will be observed (from the homogeneity property of the two functions) that the common slope of the two maps is monotonically increasing.

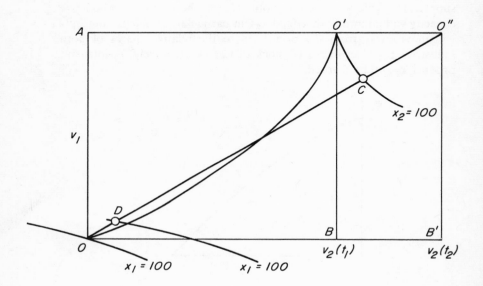

Figure 3.2. Efficient allocation of growing resources.

In economic terms, the more of the v_2-intensive good which is substituted for the other good, the higher will be the relative price of v_2 and hence its marginal physical product. At O this slope will be at its minimum, at O' or O'' at its maximum. Thus the marginal product of v_2 will be highest when only the good x_2 is produced.

Let us now consider the first box diagram $(OBO'A)$. We assume here that each industry can produce 100 units of product when using all resources of the economy optimally. In other words, the isoquants of x_1 going through O and of x_2 going through O' correspond to the level of output of 100 units. Now let us increase v_2, say, from AO' to AO''. Again O'' will lie on some isoquant of x_2 higher than 100, and another isoquant of x_1 has moved into O. On the diagonal OO'' we can now observe two points, C and D. Point C lies on the isoquant of x_2 corresponding to the output of 100 units and D on the isoquant of x_1 corresponding to the output of 100 units. The relative increases of x_1 and x_2 resulting from an increase in v_2 by $O'O''$ when nothing of the other commodity is produced are measured by OD/OO'' and CO''/OO'', respectively. The first ratio will necessarily fall short of the second since, as we have seen above, the absolute value of the slope (the equilibrium wage ratio) on the contract curve is higher at O' than at O and the production functions are homogeneous of the first order and have uniformly different factor intensities.

Thus we have established that the expansion of the transformation function will be relatively more important at the intercept on the axis of x_2. A similar construction might be employed for any point of the transformation function. Also, the box diagram analysis would prove the diminishing marginal productivity of v_2; i.e., for equal increases of this factor while the other is held constant, the axis intercepts would be closer and closer together. Hence, a typical family of transformation curves resulting from equal changes in our non-land factor would show a pattern that we have illustrated in Figure 3.3. To remind us of the

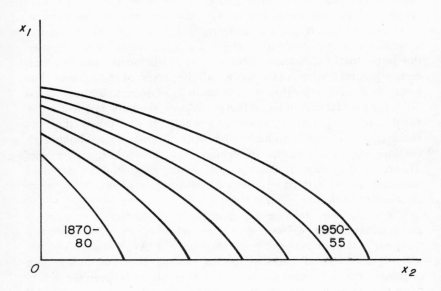

Figure 3.3.   Expanding production possibilities.

[19]

concrete purpose of the analysis, each of the production possibilities may be visualized as corresponding to the periods of our later empirical chapters (1871–1880, ... , 1951–1955).

We shall now consider the other side of the market, i.e., the conditions of demand for the two goods. To do this, let us assume that the community of the country whose production possibility is studied has a set of social preferences or social indifference loci between the two products x_1 and x_2. Although, strictly speaking, this is not necessary for the argument, let us assume that this set is nonintersecting and also has the other properties of individual indifference maps. To justify this postulate, we can assume either that each individual has the same income and the same individual preference map, or that everybody's preferences are identical and homogeneous; that is, income elasticities of every product for every individual are equal to one.

It should be observed that the social indifference contours just described can only be used in a static analysis: A set of individual or social indifferences reflects tastes as of a given instant in time. It is impossible to claim that such taste patterns would be invariant with respect to time. Tastes have certainly changed over the past 70 or 80 years.

Hence, the comparative-static model should consider a different set of indifference contours for each period. There is no precise statistical evidence about how much and in what direction tastes have changed. Only some general hypotheses concerning these changes can be made.

Although it is difficult to establish a rigorous relationship between the individual indifference contours and the social indifferences, certain general features of the former will be preserved in the latter. For instance, if Engel's law (low income elasticity of demand for necessities) holds for the majority of individual consumers, the same law will apply roughly to the group or nation as a whole. It is unlikely that the redistributive effects of an increasing national product would outweigh the low income elasticities of demand for the majority of people. This could only happen if the people gaining most from an increased national income wanted to increase consumption of necessities more than in proportion to income.

When analyzing long-period changes in equilibrium consumption and production, a new factor enters the picture which is disregarded in a short-run (static) analysis: population growth. As we move to higher and higher levels of national income (to higher social indifference contours such as depicted in Figure 3.4), the relation between the underlying individual indifference curves and those for the community will vary depending on the rate of growth of the population. This will be most clearly seen in the limiting case; if it happened that all increase in national income was matched by an equal increase in population, with identical tastes (of any kind) and constant equal shares of income, the social indifference curves would always be homogeneous whatever the individuals' patterns of taste might be. We may conclude that for a

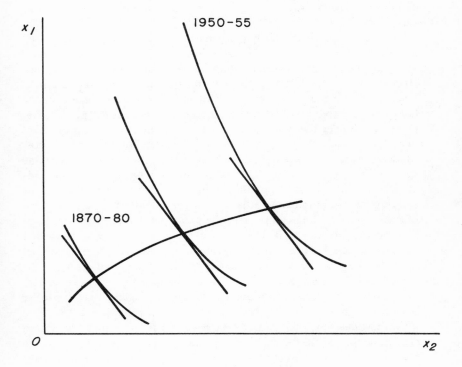

Figure 3.4. Expanding consumption.

community as a whole, a rapidly growing population will tend to soften the income (Engel's) effects usually associated with an individual's habits of consumption.

Going back to the model and to the two commodities x_1 and x_2, can we assume any particular shape for the social indifference contours? Both on a priori grounds and following from the empirical studies of the subject, we have good reason to believe that the natural resource–intensive good (x_1) will have a lower income elasticity than the labor and capital–intensive good (x_2). The income-consumption lines associated with the $x_1 x_2$ social indifference map should always bend towards the x_2 axis. As income grows, with constant prices of the two goods, relatively more will be spent on the good that uses comparatively more labor and capital than natural resources, and comparatively less on the natural resource–intensive product. One such typical map of social indifference contours has been drawn in Figure 3.4, together with an income-consumption line.

The interpretation of this map is somewhat different from that usually given to indifference curves in static analysis. Each of the above contours may again be associated with one of our periods of reference (1870–1880, ... , 1950–1955). In the short run, when population is assumed to be stationary and one of the assumptions made above holds, the contours within the static map cannot intersect; i.e., movement to a higher contour would mean an unambiguous improvement in welfare. Also, tangency between a price line (or production possibility contour) and such a social indifference contour will determine the equilibrium consumption of the community. Over the long periods of time considered here, population is not constant. New individuals entering the community and others leaving it will affect the taste pattern of the group. Nothing can prevent the social indifference contours from intersecting. Moreover, it does not make sense any more to claim that higher contours belong to higher levels of welfare. The satisfactions of individuals cannot be compared over periods as long as 10 years.

Our main concern, however, is not to evaluate the levels of welfare of a growing economy at different points in time, but to establish the equilibrium points of production and trading. And this can still be done if we assume the following: At each time period examined, certain conditions prevail in the economy and can be taken as constant in the short run; no important change in population can take place, and tastes of different individuals are assumed unchanged. To these conditions corresponds a certain pattern of social tastes. Each of the dated contours of Figure 3.4 then typifies the particular conditions of the period chosen. For convenience, only one contour for each period has been drawn. These contours can no longer be numbered (as is usually done to express the ordinal preference of higher over lower contours). Also, nothing can guarantee that they would not intersect. Nevertheless, we can still expect that this map would again show a low income elasticity of x_1, provided that this is the case for all underlying "short-run" sets of tastes.

Thus we are now equipped with a set of transformation loci between x_1 and x_2 and with a long-range indifference map. With each date we can associate one transformation curve and a set of indifference curves. From our assumption of constant returns to scale and different factor intensities of the two production functions, it follows that all the transformation curves will be convex upward. From our earlier discussion, it follows that these loci cannot intersect. On the other hand, the social indifference contours for each particular date are convex downward, do not intersect, and can be numbered going outward from the origin, a higher number always standing for a higher level of satisfaction. Hence, it will be in the interests of the community to move as far as possible in the northeast direction, given its productive capacity in a particular period. Competitive markets will guarantee such solutions.

For each period there will be one equilibrium point defined by the tangency of the transformation line and one of the infinity of social indifference contours of the period. Thus, by combining Figure 3.3 and Figure 3.4, we can construct the expansion path ξ of production and consumption for a closed economy. This is shown in Figure 3.5.

Only the indifference contours belonging to the equilibrium positions have been drawn in the diagram. Both the expansion of the production block and the assumed nature of tastes work to pull the ξ curve (expansion path) closer to the x_2 axis. The expansion path ξ need not be a monotonic curve such as the one drawn in the diagram. From period to period, population, tastes, and production possibilities might have changed to such an extent as to reverse its direction. Over long periods of time, ξ may be taken as a general indicator of the path.

As usual, the absolute value of the slope of the tangency common to the indifference curve and to the transformation function expresses the price ratio of the two commodities at the given period. Two such tangencies, AA and BB, have been drawn in the diagram for the beginning and the end of the period considered. If the nation as a whole had a unit-elastic demand for both goods at each period and at each level of income, with the production of the labor-capital-intensive good expanding comparatively faster than that of the land-intensive good, there would be a tendency for the former to become cheaper. But according to our presumption that with increasing national per capita income relatively more of x_2 will be demanded, this cheapening effect may be softened or completely offset. Thus, while the changing production possibility and tastes co-operate in their effect on the physical expansion path, they have opposite (canceling) effects on relative prices.[7]

[7] We shall see later in our empirical chapters that this actually occurred in the American economy: While relative prices of extractive and other goods were not changing very much, the composition of consumption turned drastically in favor of the latter.

Let us now turn to the actual problem of this section and give up the assumption of a closed economy. We shall assume elasticities of foreign supply and of demand to be infinite over the entire period. At a given relative price of the two commodities, the outside world is willing to supply or take any amount of x_1 or x_2. In geometrical terms, we may now draw in the x_1x_2 plane a family of price lines parallel to each other.

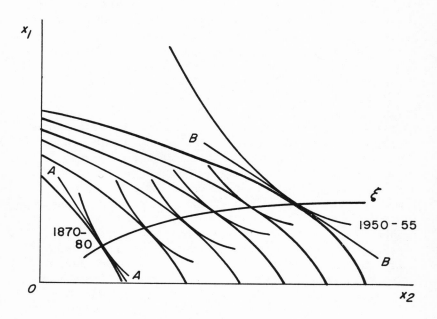

Figure 3.5. Expanding production and consumption without trade.

Each period t_i defines one transformation contour and one indifference map. One contour of this map will touch but not intersect one of the infinity of price lines which, at the same time, is tangent to the relevant transformation curve. Thus two points of tangency are defined for each t_i. The first is a point on the consumption path of the community; the second is a point of production. Varying t over the period under examination will generate two loci: ξ, which connects all production points, and η, which connects all consumption points. The differences between consumption and production at each period of time determine the amounts and direction of foreign trade. The construction of the two curves is shown in Figure 3.6.

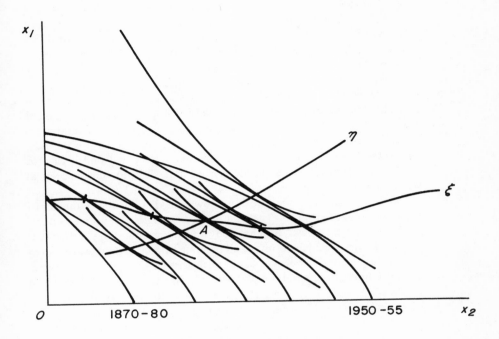

Figure 3.6. Expanding production and consumption with international trade.

The diagram has been drawn to illustrate most closely what has actually happened in the American economy over the last hundred years or so. As the shape of the first production block indicates, the economy has been relatively abundantly supplied with land. Hence, the land-intensive commodity has been exported and the other commodity imported.[8] As time passed, increases in capital and in population gradually rendered natural resources more and more scarce. The productive

[8] In drawing this parallel between our model and the American economy, we of course have to be aware of the fact that not two but a large number of commodities are being produced and traded. Hence, we may think of our two commodities as two physical index numbers aggregating all commodities defined as capital-labor-intensive and land-intensive, respectively.

potential of the economy expanded faster in favor of capital-labor-intensive goods; so comparative advantage followed the same direction. As a result, exports of x_1 and imports of x_2 were continuously reduced until the United States changed from a net exporter of resource products to a net importer. Of course, consideration of actual trade data would never reveal a point of autarchy, such as A in Figure 3.6. It is the structure rather than absolute levels of trade that is changing in the real world. An index of *net* resource requirements of trade would show such a pattern.[9]

To study the impact of changing factor supplies, we have assumed in what precedes an unchanging terms-of-trade ratio. In the real world this will never be exactly the case, and it was not the case for the United States over the past 85 years. Relative prices of primary and manufactured products have been changing in one direction in certain periods, and in the opposite direction in others. The reader will find it easy to incorporate such changes of the terms of trade into our theoretical representation.

Using our simple model, we may now consider briefly the impact of changing technology or total productivity on the natural resource requirements of foreign trade.[10] In general, by improved technology, or technological change, we mean a shift of all or some isoquants downward and to the left. In our case, we may distinguish three situations: land-saving, capital-labor-saving, and finally neutral changes. They are shown in Figures 3.7a, b, and c, where P_0 and P_1 correspond to a given isoquant before and after technological change, respectively, while v_1 again stands for the land factor and v_2 for the capital-labor factor of production.

The dividing line between the two extreme cases may be drawn as follows: A neutral technological improvement is one in which (with unchanged factor prices) factor proportions remain constant for the same level of output. Thus a homothetic shift of an isoquant map would always be neutral. If (again with unchanged relative factor prices) the proportion of land to the labor-capital factor increases, we call the innovation labor-capital-saving. Of course, a change in technology can

[9] E.g., see the indexes estimated in Chapter 7.

[10] Our use of "technological change" and "change of total productivity" as synonymous concepts may appear to be unusual. Both concepts are loosely used by economists to describe changes of efficiency, i.e., changes of the production function as opposed to movements on a single production surface. There have been recent attempts to measure changing efficiency empirically, by a single index; the index is then often designated a "total factor productivity." In our present discussion we usually speak of technological change, although we use the term "total productivity" in our later empirical discussion (Chapter 8). It should be kept in mind that both terms refer to the same phenomenon.

be both labor-capital and land-saving, depending on the region of the production function in which the firm operates (i.e., depending on the relative factor prices).

In order to study the impact of technological change on the equilibrium trading and production points of the economy as a whole, let us now consider the transformation function.

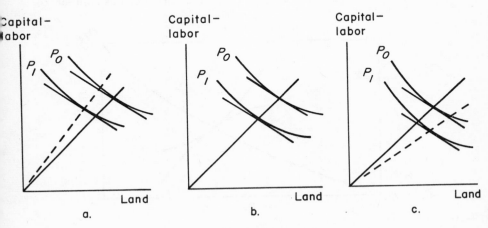

Figure 3.7. Different types of technological progress.

The general effect of technological improvement in one of the two industries can most easily be seen in our familiar box diagram. Again assume unit-homogeneous production functions of the two sectors. A neutral innovation takes place in, say, the labor-capital-intensive industry (x_2). Under such conditions, nothing has changed in the box shown in Figure 3.8 except the numbering of the isoquants belonging to x_2. Assuming a 10% increase in over-all productivity, the isoquant for $x_2 = 7$ will now bear the number 7.7, etc. (as shown in the diagram); that is, the x_2 industry will now produce, with any combination of productive factors indicated by the isoquant, 7.7 units of output rather than the 7 units produced previously.

The contract curve in the box diagram can now be translated into two different transformation functions. The new contour is a 10% rightward blowup of the original one. Obviously, the position of the x_1 intercept is unchanged. At any other level of output of x_2 our economy will be able to produce more of x_1 than previously, since some resources

[27]

have been liberated for use in this industry. The original and the new transformation curves are depicted in Figure 3.9 by the contours A and B, respectively.

By a similar argument we may deduce the shape and position of the transformation curves when innovation in the x_2 production is either land- or labor-capital-biased (and no change of efficiency took place in x_1). The reader may determine for himself that the former will result in a curve such as contour C and the latter in a curve such as contour D.

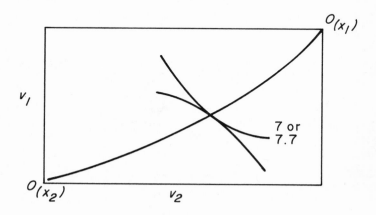

Figure 3.8. Efficient allocation of resources and technological progress.

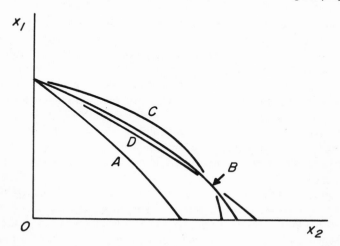

Figure 3.9. The production possibility and different types of innovation.

In other words, compared with the neutral-innovation line, the land-saving innovation will give rise to a curve more bowed out than B, while a labor-capital-saving innovation will make the contour comparatively flatter. From the assumptions of non-intersection of isoquants before and after technological change and of convexity, it follows that the new transformation curves cannot intersect the original curve.

Considering now the information which we may expect from empirical sources, it would be immaterial to consider all three types of technological advance for one of the industries when analyzing the impact of innovation or changing technology on foreign trade.

The last step to be made is to combine, as before, the transformation maps with the long-run indifference map defined above. As can be observed, there is a striking similarity between technological improvement and disproportional growth of different types of resources. Let us simply note that a pattern exactly identical to that depicted in Figure 3.6 would be obtained with unchanged endowments of all resources and technological improvement in both sectors, but faster in x_2 than in x_1. In the limiting case, in which technology was stationary in the resource sector and advanced only in the other sector in such a way as to yield the same incomes in the different periods as did growth of factor endowments (see Figure 3.6), the effect on trade would be even stronger than that of changing resource supplies. This is illustrated in Figure 3.10, in which an indifference map (as in Figure 3.6) and a similar original position of the production possibility curve have been used.

Again we assume infinite elasticities of supply and demand for the rest of the world. It can be seen that with the same world prices as before, the expansion path of consumption (η) would remain unchanged. The production path, on the other hand, would decline more sharply, since no blowup of the production block has taken place in the upward direction. Thus, if consumption in each period of time is the same as in the previous case (autonomous growth of the capital-labor factor), international trade will be relatively more important than before.

If we now simultaneously consider the effects of technology and disproportionate growth of resource supplies, we can easily see that they are additive. While relatively faster technological progress in the non-resource industries would accelerate the rate at which the structure of foreign trade is changing because of growing non-land factor supplies, a relative technological bias in favor of farming and mining would tend to offset this effect.

It is obvious that we could hardly find a case in the real world which would be exactly reflected by our diagram, i.e., one in which no advance in the resource industries is coupled with growing total productivity in the rest of the economy. Perhaps French agriculture before World War II provides a good approximation. In general, however, as we shall see in Chapter 8, United States technological advance has taken place in both sectors simultaneously although the rates of change have been different.

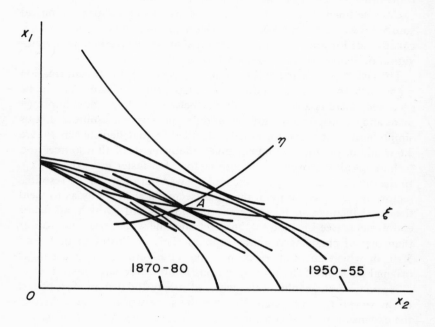

Figure 3.10. Technological growth and international trade.

It would be possible to extend the application of our model to show several other reasons for the change in the resource structure of international trade. For example, we might consider the effect of changing tastes, and changes of resources and productivity in foreign countries. An important change in the nature of foreign trade can also be shown to follow if, with increasing returns to scale, innovations in different export industries are strongly biased in opposite directions.[11] These cases, however, are too subtle, and information to prove or disprove their existence in the real world is lacking.

[11] Note that under such conditions the transformation curve can change from convex to concave or vice versa.

[30]

4

The Factor-Proportions Theory of Foreign Trade

ONE other theoretical matter should be treated before we turn to the empirical section of this book. It concerns the factor-proportions theory of international trade. In Chapter 9 we shall use empirical data to examine the relative abundance of productive factors in the United States and in the rest of the world. Economic theory dealing with this relation — currently associated with the names of Heckscher and Ohlin — does not, however, lend itself directly to the treatment of the present problem. Actually, rigorous treatment of Ohlin's theorems uses only a two-factor, two-commodity model. Because it is the natural resource factor of production that concerns us and because there is virtually an infinite number of products traded between the United States and the rest of the world, a somewhat closer examination of the general case is in order.

Consideration of *competitive* imports rather than total imports in evaluating a country's factor abundance also may not be quite justified. In particular, this holds if we deal with natural resources. Actually we should not ignore — as does Professor Leontief — the portion of imports which does not compete with domestic production. In the extreme case, a country importing nothing but complementary products may be said to reveal no scarcity of resources; yet common sense will indicate that in such a situation relative scarcity of certain productive factors is most severe.

Let us consider a two-country world (such as the United States and the rest of the world combined). Each of these two countries produces a large number of commodities from three different factors of production: land, capital, and labor. An identical pool of technological knowledge is shared by both countries, and all production functions are homogeneous of the first order. The tastes of both regions are identical and homogeneous. Transportation is cost-free, and international exchange

31

of commodities is not impeded by any restrictive policies of either country. The reader who is familiar with the factor-proportions theory of international trade will recognize that the assumptions made thus far are at least as general as those customarily made. Moreover, we may assume that country A owns capital, labor, and land in proportions of three to two to one, while country B is endowed with the different resources in proportions of one to two to three. Because all production functions are smooth and everywhere convex to the origin, and because both countries tend to maximize real income, all resources will be fully employed. It follows from our assumptions that once international exchange of goods is permitted, both countries will consume all products in identical proportions. Further, we may assume that the factor endowments of the two countries are such that if they trade they will consume not only proportional but identical quantities of every product. Such an assumption will not affect the generality of our conclusions.

Concerning the nature of the production functions in the pool of technological knowledge, we shall make two alternative sets of assumptions, crucial for our later analysis.

> *Hypothesis 1:* The large number of production techniques employed in producing the many commodities are of uniform factor intensities with respect to one another.[1] Moreover, among the products, there is no particular tendency for any factor of production to be complementary to another one. In other words, the probability that we can draw from our large population of techniques one which would always use, say, land in conjunction with capital is equal to the probability that we can draw a product in which land and labor are combined in similar quantities.

> *Hypothesis 2:* The second case corresponds to a situation where one factor, such as land, tends to be complementary to another factor of production, such as capital, in the majority of productive processes used by the two economies.

Let us consider the case described by our general assumptions and hypothesis 1. The factor-proportions theory of international trade postulates that a country will export the product using relatively more of its abundant factor. A similar statement in terms of commodities

---

[1] I.e., if product x_1 is relatively land-intensive with respect to a product x_2 for one set of factor prices, then this relation must hold, in a competitive equilibrium, for any other set of factor prices.

would become rather cumbersome if large numbers of products are traded. Consequently, let us rephrase the theory in the following way: A country relatively well supplied with a given factor of production will be a net exporter of the services of this factor. Or in the case of three factors of production we may say that the factor requirements of exports will reflect the relative factor endowments of the country, while imports will reflect the endowments of the other country.

It is virtually impossible to provide a rigorous proof of these propositions. Nevertheless, we shall make an attempt at a partial demonstration and leave the rest of the proof to the common sense and the intuition of the reader. It has been shown by James Meade, Paul Samuelson, and other writers that under the assumptions made here, if a large number of commodities are traded and only a few factors of production are used, prices (measured in terms of any commodity) of productive factors will be equalized between trading partners. It then follows from the homogeneity of all production functions that factors will be used in both countries in identical proportions for each commodity produced in both countries. It is clear that under these conditions each country will find it most efficient to produce most of the particular goods which, at least approximately, use factors of production in proportions similar to the proportions of its own factor endowments. Those will be the commodities entering international trade in the greatest amounts. Products using factors of production in different proportions from those of the factor endowment of either country will tend to be produced by both countries, and the inducement to trade such commodities will be smaller.

But if the trade tends to have this particular commodity structure, then it should also be clear that the requirements of productive factors contained in total exports and imports will be similar to the factor endowments of the two countries.

So far we have considered the case where there is no particular tendency among the multitude of commodities for one factor of production to be complementary to or substitute for another factor (hypothesis 1). Let us now relax this assumption and deal with a case in which, for example, capital and natural resources are two strongly complementary factors for the large majority of products (hypothesis 2 above). In this case our conclusion regarding the factor structure of foreign trade may no longer hold.

Earlier in this chapter we made the assumption that country A is endowed with capital, labor, and land in proportions of three to two to one, while country B's factor supplies can be ranked in the opposite

order. Under hypothesis 1 we should expect the relative factor requirements of country A's exports to imports to assume the order[2]

$$\frac{C_x}{C_m} > \frac{L_x}{L_m} > \frac{T_x}{T_m} \tag{4.1}$$

Under hypothesis 2, this order may be reversed, or at least the
differences between the above ratios reduced. If the land factor happens
to be scarce in country A, then A's imports will contain an important
portion of natural resource requirements. But owing to the fact that
natural resources cannot be exploited without a good deal of investment,
the capital requirements of imports may have to be quite substantial in
spite of the fact that country B is relatively scarce in capital; and this
may produce a ranking such as

$$\frac{L_x}{L_m} > \frac{C_x}{C_m} > \frac{T_x}{T_m} \tag{4.2}$$

The empirical findings presented in Chapter 9 indicate that this situation
has a good deal of relevance for the United States.

[2] The letters C, L, T stand for capital, labor, and land requirements, respectively,
while the subscripts correspond to exports (x) and imports (m). It is immaterial
whether we speak of value or physical requirements, because factor prices of each
factor in both countries are expected to be equal.

5

Direct Resource Requirements
of American Foreign Trade

Introduction

Thus far we have discussed some of the most important theoretical issues related to the topic of our study. We have delineated the principal concepts with which we want to deal, and theories which either explain or clarify the phenomena which we shall study.

In this and subsequent chapters, we shall approach the real world. Using the qualitative and quantitative information at hand, or data derived from it, we shall describe as faithfully as possible past events and explain them wherever possible.

This chapter presents crude data concerning the resource content of American foreign trade. We shall first consider the share of principal classes of resource products in total American exports and imports. Their fluctuation in terms of value and volume as well as changing unit values over the past 85 years will also be examined. Moreover, we shall concentrate on the *competitive* and *complementary* components of American imports, and show in more detail how the commodity composition of resource product imports has been changing. The concluding section of this chapter will deal with the regional distribution of this country's foreign trade in natural resource products.

The Paley Report[1] provides a key, or starting point, for our statistical analysis. Its introductory section[2] stresses the important historical fact of the changing structure of American foreign trade. Figure 5.1 illustrates this trend.

Although 70% of United States exports in 1820 consisted of crude materials, this share was not higher than 25% in the five years immediately following the Second World War. Clearly, if it had not been

[1] Report to the President by the President's Materials Policy Commission, *Resources for Freedom* (Washington, D.C., U.S. Government Printing Office, 1952).
[2] *Ibid.*, Vol. 1, p. 16.

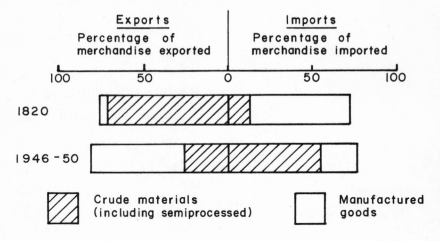

Figure 5.1. Our exports of 1820 are our imports now.

for the urgent need for American basic products in the rest of the world in those five years, the figure might have been well below 25%. On the import side, the opposite pattern will be observed. The share of crude materials increased from 12% of total imports in 1820 to more than 50% in the period 1946–1950. Crude foodstuffs, to which attention will also be given in our study, demonstrate a similar pattern, though less pronounced.

The changing resource structure of American exports and imports is even more revealing and interesting if viewed in detail. Between 1870 and 1955, the trend in favor of relatively increasing net exports of manufactures was by no means uniform. The structure of American exports over the 85 years under consideration was also not a symmetrical mirror-image of the structure of imports.

There are several explanatory hypotheses to be tested in this and the following chapters: changing technology, increasing resource scarcity, changing tastes, impact of wars, falling transportation costs, etc. On the other hand, we may be able to judge from our findings the relative resource position of the United States in the world economy.

Statistical Method

Chapter 2 was devoted to theoretical considerations related to the measure of the natural resource content of a given bill of goods (total

[36]

exports or total imports in our case). We shall therefore restrict ourselves here to a brief summary of previous findings and shall then proceed to the purely statistical implications of the problem.

In Chapter 2 we argued on theoretical grounds that economic rent (i.e., the wage of the natural resource factor of production) would serve best as an index of natural resource content. As a variable derived directly from the general equilibrium setting, economic rent is the truest possible measure of the relative scarcity of the particular type of land to which it is attached. In fact, in the final analysis we *must* be interested in this quality of economic rent — more so perhaps than would be necessary for the price of any other economic factor which, unlike land, is reproducible.

And yet it is impossible to use this index. The statistical information at hand is far from adequate in order to yield meaningful estimates of economic rent. Moreover, in agriculture, the impossibility of separating land from capital invested in it and the difficulty of imputing rent to different types of crops make such estimation extremely difficult. As the reader may realize, it is even more difficult to construct meaningful estimates of rent for nonreplaceable resources. Here even a workable definition of the particular factor of production is missing.

Consequently, we have turned to a substitute for economic rent, which, though theoretically inferior, is far more workable statistically. Among the alternative measures, the value of resource products appears the most suitable for several reasons.

"Resource products" we understand to be commodities which are nearest to the initial stages of the productive process. In all such commodities, land (or natural resources) is used as an "active" input; that is, the productive contribution of land is more than just the supplying of space for production. Thus, farming, forestry, and mining will be defined as resource industries rather than housing, manufacturing, and transportation.

Of course, the real resource input — the share of economic rent in total unit value of product — will vary considerably between different resource products. For farming production as a whole, Professor Schultz[3] finds this share to be around 25%. He also claims that this proportion has remained fairly constant over the past 50 years. The value of bauxite in its natural form is quite negligible compared with that of the labor and capital inputs necessary for its extraction; the same applies to many different resource products which use low-grade lands. Crops

[3] T. W. Schultz, *The Economic Organization of Agriculture* (New York, McGraw-Hill, 1953), p. 137.

grown on Ricardian "marginal land" also fall into this group.[4] On the whole, however, there is a strong likelihood that the natural resource content of these commodities is substantially greater than that of more highly fabricated commodities in which the productive contribution of land enters only indirectly.

Obviously, the actual definition of these sectors will be somewhat arbitrary. It is difficult to draw an exact line between active and non-active use of natural resources in certain types of industries. Since similar difficulties, often more serious, arise everywhere in economics,[5] we need not be unduly disturbed.

In dealing with problems of natural resources, Resources for the Future, Inc., has used the classification of the Bureau of Labor Statistics to define 21 out of the 192 sectors of the United States economy as extractive, or resource-product-producing. In Chapter 7, in which we study the direct and indirect requirements of American foreign trade, we shall conform to this classification.

In the present chapter, however, we make use of the traditional breakdown in which the United States foreign trade data are recorded: namely, crude materials, crude foodstuffs, semi-manufactures, finished foodstuffs, and manufactures. The first two classes correspond to our definition of resource products. They cover almost exactly the 21 sectors of the Resources for the Future definition mentioned above. The statistical data are available for a period of over 130 years and for most of the period are presented as five- or ten-year averages, which are more suitable for this study of long-run changes.[6] Wherever necessary, such averages have been computed from yearly figures.

Before we approach the actual results, a few words of general caution concerning our index may be useful. We have already noticed that the natural resource content of the resource commodities will be quite different for different products. Moreover, resource content of individual commodities is likely to change over time owing to changing factor prices and changing technology. Hence, a changed share of resource products in total trade does not necessarily mean that the resource content of trade has changed. It is possible that while the relative value of resource commodities has gone down, more resource-intensive commodities have entered the aggregate, or that the resource content of any given commodity may have changed. Consequently, if we want to

---

[4] Note that Professor Schultz's estimate is an average.

[5] E.g., the difference between capital and consumer goods.

[6] For discussion of sources, and methods of computation, see the appendix to this chapter.

believe our indicator of resource intensiveness, we have to trust the law of large numbers. Our index would be perfect only if all resource commodities were produced from land alone, and all other commodities from other productive factors alone (not using any of the resource commodities as intermediate products). But more was said about these problems in Chapter 2.

Another difficulty arises from the possibility that a shift in the share of resource products in total trade would be matched by an opposite shift in the semi-manufactures, which do not enter our index. In order to check this, we have also recorded the group of semi-manufactures in our statistics. Moreover, we shall eliminate this possibility in Chapter 7, where indirect inputs are also considered.

Findings

Values

Figure 5.2 presents the percentage shares of raw materials, crude foodstuffs, finished foodstuffs, semi-manufactures, and manufactured goods in total American exports since 1870. At the same time the index of the value of total exports is given at the top of the chart.

At the beginning of the period the structure of exports was typically that of a country in an early stage of industrialization. Almost 60% of all exports consisted of natural resource products (crude foodstuffs and raw materials). Exports of finished foodstuffs which usually require only simple productive processes (e.g., flour-milling) represented another important part of American exports. It is in these groups that we find the comparative advantage of this country. Natural resources were the dominant factor of production determining this advantage vis-à-vis Europe, America's principal customer during the period. Manufactured products and semi-manufactures stood for only 14% and 5% of American exports, respectively.

On the side of natural resource products, cotton and tobacco in Class 1 and wheat and corn in Class 2 dominated the exports of the United States. Coal and crude petroleum gained in importance only later.

Taking a long view of the 85-year period, we observe a pronounced increase in the share of manufactured goods, and a diminishing share of resource products, reflecting the changing comparative advantage of the United States.

While both raw materials and crude foodstuffs fell in relative importance in the last three decades of the past century, the other three

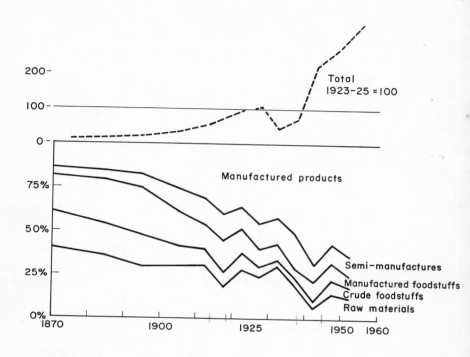

Figure 5.2. Index of total value of American exports and percentage shares by economic classes. (*For sources, see appendix to this chapter.*)

classes gained. Note the increasing share of finished foodstuffs during the period; only from the beginning of this century did this class decline continuously in relative importance. Manufactured goods, on the other hand, gained only slightly in the first 30 years of the period and did not increase rapidly until later. From the turn of the century until the First World War, the share of crude materials in total exports remained stationary. With a rapidly growing income abroad, particularly in Europe, exports of crude and manufactured foodstuffs were marked by an important relative decline, falling from 45 to 24% of total exports. Low income elasticities of food, protection in Europe, and industrialization in the United States seem to be the best explanation for this decline.

[40]

The two world wars had similar impact on the structure of American exports. The needs of the fighting allies caused an abnormal increase in the export of manufactured goods and finished foodstuffs, at the expense of other commodities. We observe a similar drop in the share of resource products exported in times of high prosperity. In the late 1920's, the share of manufactured goods exported increased beyond what the trend would indicate. This time, however, exports of semi-manufactures (rather than finished foodstuffs) also increased sharply. This result could be expected because of high levels of income and the comparatively higher income elasticity of these two commodity classes.

With a fall of almost 60% of the total value of exports in the depression, raw materials returned to their relative level of the beginning of the century, while foreign demand for American crude foodstuffs slackened to a low of 4% of total exports. The demand remained at this low level until 1945, but increased somewhat after World War II as a result of world food shortages and the consequent United States economic assistance. Owing mainly to an increased domestic demand during the war and also to the necessity of saving shipping space, we find raw materials falling to an all-time low of 6% of total exports in the first half of the 1940's. Once world demand recovered from its postwar distortion, the general trends of the previous 50 years were again continued.

Let us now give attention to imports. Because of the changing comparative advantage of the United States, we might expect that the structure of American imports would have changed rather symmetrically with that of exports — that is, that there would have been a rapid movement of shares in favor of resource products and away from manufactured goods. On first examination of Figure 5.3 we see that this was not so. If we take an over-all view of the 85 years, we can see two important differences. First, the rate of change appears to be somewhat less pronounced for imports than for exports; and second, by the time of the First World War we observe a general stabilization of the share taken by resource products in total imports.

Resource products increased from 33% to about one half of total imports during the first half of our period and held roughly at this level throughout the remaining four decades. With a rapidly increasing demand for industrial materials such as wool, silk, rubber, hides, and skins, raw materials made their greatest gain prior to the First World War; imports of crude foodstuffs declined somewhat in relative importance. The two classes which lost most during this period were finished manufactures and manufactured foodstuffs. Both were affected by rapidly increasing domestic competition.

[41]

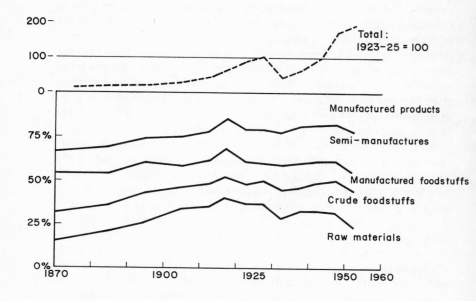

Figure 5.3. Index of total value of American imports and percentage shares
by economic classes. (*For sources, see appendix to this chapter.*)

No strong impact of war on the structure of trade will be found in
American imports. While in the First World War demand for foreign
crude materials increased somewhat above its normal share, the
Second World War left the composition of imports virtually unchanged.
The only class which increased over the entire period was that of semi-
manufactures, dominated by metals for industrial use.

In general, it seems that changing comparative advantage was the
principal determinant of the structure of trade, on the side of exports.
With respect to imports, on the other hand, propensities to import (or
income elasticities) were also important. A good illustration of the
relatively low income elasticity at work will be found in the Great
Depression; only crude and manufactured foodstuffs increased their
share between 1926–30 and 1931–35. Over the same period, raw
materials fell from 37 to 29% of the total value of imports; at the same
time relative prices of crude materials and of foodstuffs remained virtually unchanged.

But we would not give the whole story of American imports of resource products if we relied only on the comparatively low income
elasticity of the majority of commodities which enter this class. While
the share of resource products remained virtually unchanged over the
past four decades, important changes were taking place within the
aggregate. Certain commodities were growing in importance, while
others declined in relative importance. If the forces which made some
commodities lose their relative importance had not been present, the
aggregate value of resource products imported would certainly have
moved in the direction which we might have expected owing to the
changing comparative advantage of this country.

In Figure 5.4 we show the shares (in terms of value at current prices)

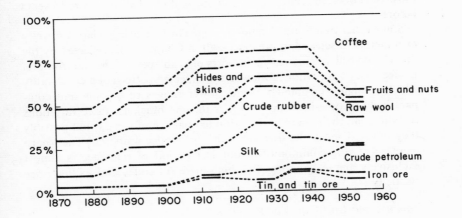

Figure 5.4. United States imports of principal resource products for selected
periods, as percentage of total listed, current values. (*For sources, see
appendix to this chapter.*)

of nine leading resource commodities imported into the United States
over the 85-year period. It should be noted that these nine products
cover about two thirds of the total of imported resource products. Over
the entire period this proportion was remarkably stable.

Although the trends revealed by our chart are quite familiar, they
still deserve our attention. Chapter 8 is devoted to the impact of technological change in different productive sectors on the resource structure of American foreign trade. The most interesting trends of our

chart are also a result of technological change — but of another variety. While in Chapter 8 we deal with shifting isoquants, we encounter here technological substitution of one material for another (change of axes in the factor-output space).

Natural rubber and silk provide·the two most striking examples. But hides and skins as well as raw wool tell a similar story. Both crude rubber and silk were increasing in relative importance until 1930, as might have been expected from the comparatively higher income elasticities of the products for which they are used. Crude rubber further increased its relative share into the 1930's, while imports of silk declined, owing to the introduction of synthetic substitutes and to depressed incomes during the same decade. The technological substitution which occurred during World War II practically eliminated imports of silk and reduced those of rubber, in relative terms, to one half of what they were 15 years before.

Some other trends are also interesting. The increasing relative scarcity of minerals (discussed in greater detail in Chapter 8) is reflected by the "new" and quickly increasing imports of crude petroleum and iron ore. Coffee has, on the whole, followed the expected pattern of a commodity which is highly income-elastic for lower ranges of income and comparatively income-inelastic in higher income brackets. Price variations certainly had their share in the exhibited pattern of trends; but possibly they affected most the relative value of coffee imports. The sharp increase of this commodity in our last period of reference is almost exclusively due to "abnormally" high prices of coffee and its low price elasticity.

*Volumes and Unit Values of Resource Products
and Supply and Demand Conditions*

Having examined the changing structure of American foreign trade in terms of value, we now want to see to what extent these changes were due to changing prices and to what extent to changing physical volumes. We shall consider here the two classes of resource products — raw materials and crude foodstuffs — and total trade. Figures 5.5 and 5.6 contain the results, which are all index numbers based on 1923–25 = 100.

All statistics for the period following 1913 are taken from official United States documents. We have estimated the volume and unit-value indexes of "raw materials" and "crude foodstuffs" for the earlier period. Unit-value estimates for total exports and imports are based on the calculations of T. J. Kreps, and cover the period 1879–1913.[7]

[7] For additional discussion of sources and methods see the appendix to this chapter.

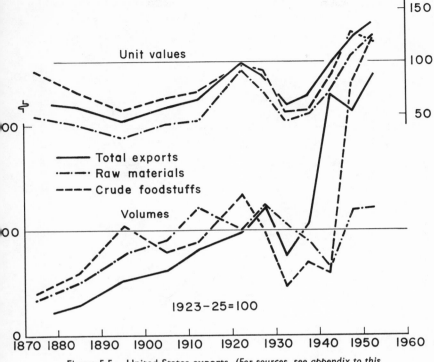

Figure 5.5. United States exports. (*For sources, see appendix to this chapter.*)

The coverage of our estimates for exports and imports of crude food-stuffs and exports of raw materials is quite satisfactory (60 to 80%). That for imported raw materials is inferior because of lack of information and the great variety of materials imported. Consequently, estimates of unit value and volume for this class should be taken with more caution. With a low coverage, an important fall in the price of silk (included in our estimate) during the period may cause serious distortion.

The results of this section will be useful in examining variations of supply and demand over shorter periods of time. In this case, distortion and loss of information of the index-number variety are less likely.

American export as well as import unit values show similar long-range patterns. After a peak in the 1870's, they first declined and then increased again in a long swing covering almost 60 years, reaching a

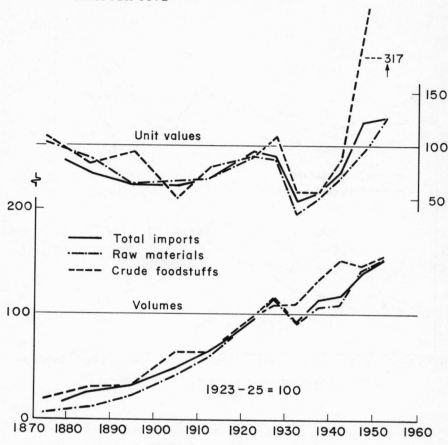

Figure 5.6. United States imports. (*For sources, see appendix to this chapter.*)

trough around the turn of the century and another high during the twenties. A similar though accelerated wave is observable in the remaining 30 years, with an all-time high manifested during the last decade. Through these long-range movements, export unit values gained more than those of imports. Whatever its meaning may be, the United States gain in net barter terms of trade over the last 80 years of our study was above 50%.

Taking the trend of total import unit values as a standard of comparison, we observe that the imports of crude foodstuffs and raw materials were both comparatively expensive in the early decades.

Around 1900, however, both series of unit values declined to the level of the unit values of all imports and remained close to that general level through the twenties. Unit values of crude foodstuffs later advanced as compared with the average unit value and, owing to the extremely high coffee prices of the postwar years, reached a level two and a half times higher than that of total imports. Raw materials, on the other hand, lagged somewhat behind the general trend until the early thirties and only caught up with total import unit values (i.e., with the parity of 1923–25) in recent years.

On the export side, more regularity than that for imports can be observed between the trends of the unit values of total exports, and of the two classes of resource products. With the exception of the most recent period, the direction of change was the same for all three series throughout the 85 years. In the long run, prices of American exports of food (primarily wheat) declined in comparison with the general level of all export prices. Raw materials unit values, on the other hand, gained in the first five decades and declined as compared with all exports in the last 25 years, but less than did the unit values of crude foodstuffs.

On the whole, we can conclude that variations in price of resource products relative to the general price levels of exports and imports were not very important. This means that if we took as a measure of the resource content valuations at constant prices, we would find changes in the structure of American foreign trade similar to those shown in Figures 5.2 and 5.3. There is one possible exception to this generalization: The unit value of crude foodstuffs after World War II was so high compared with the average unit value that we would have recorded a decrease rather than an increase of relative importance of this class in total imports if valuation at constant prices had been used.

Let us now turn our attention to the period-to-period variation, which is statistically more reliable. We have twelve observations of ten- and five-year periods for each of our series (i.e., unit values and volumes of exports and imports of raw materials, crude foodstuffs, and all commodities combined). Hence, eleven comparisons can be obtained for each.

Using the simplest notions of partial equilibrium analysis, we want to determine the predominance of the impact of supply and/or demand on the changing conditions in the markets of resource products.[8] We again take the unit values and volumes of total trade as an indication

[8] It is impossible to find from price and quantity data the exact position or shape of the supply and demand schedules. All such schedules change with time. Nevertheless, we usually associate an increase of price and quantity with an increased

[47]

of the general trends. The changes in unit values and volumes of resource products are measured relative to these trends. Using $S+$ and $S-$, $D+$ and $D-$, for dominant increase and fall of supply, dominant increase and fall of demand, respectively, we obtain the results for the eleven comparisons shown in Table 5.1.

On the whole, we observe stronger variation in the conditions of

TABLE 5.1

Effects of Supply and Demand on United States Trade in
Resource Products

Period Compared with Period Immediately Preceding	Exports		Imports	
	Raw Materials	Crude Foodstuffs	Raw Materials	Crude Foodstuffs
(1871–1880)				
1881–1890	$D-$	$D-$	$S-$	$D-$
1891–1900	$D-$	$S-$	$S+$	$S-$
1901–1910	$D+$	$D-$	$D+$	$S+$
1911–1915	$S+$	$D-$	$S+$	$S-$
1921–1925	$S-$	$S+$	$S-$	$S+$
1926–1930	$D-$	$D-$	*	$S-$
1931–1935	$S+$	$S-$	$D-$	$S+$
1936–1940	$S-$	$S+$	$S-$	$D-$
1941–1945	$D-$	$D-$	*	$D+$
1946–1950	$D+$	$D+$	$S+$	$S-$
1951–1955	$S-$	$S+$	$S-$	$S-$

*No dominance of either supply or demand observed.

demand, a fall of price and an increase of quantity with increasing supply, etc. The symbols employed in Table 5.1 correspond to the four cases below:

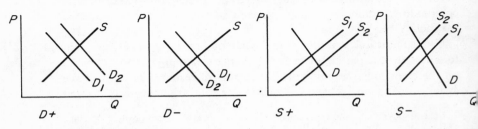

P: price Q: quantity

supply and demand in the rest of the world than in the United States. This is mainly apparent in the case of American imports of resource products. Only in three cases out of eleven for imports of crude foodstuffs and in two out of nine for imports of raw materials does D appear in our table. In all remaining cases foreign supply dominated the relative changes of price and quantity. Relative shifts of the supply schedules to the left were more frequent for both classes of resource products than were those to the right.

Foreign demand enters the picture in six cases out of eleven in exports of both crude foodstuffs and raw materials. In the former class all but one shift were in the direction of smaller demand. Increasing demand for American raw materials dominated the market only twice.

In several cases the results conform to our general knowledge of particular markets. The only recorded increase of demand for American crude foodstuffs relative to the average took place after World War II, and it was followed by an oversupply in the subsequent five years. A similar pattern would probably be found for the period immediately following World War I. Unfortunately, data for this period are not available. The case of exports of raw materials in the first postwar years was similar; but supply seems to have adjusted differently in the following five years.

The alternating shifts of supply of foreign foodstuffs also remind us of a familiar phenomenon. Note that the bulk of this class consists of coffee. Its period of adjustment to the requirements of increased demand is known to be long and often to overshoot the mark. We may argue that rubber, and possibly silk, had a similar impact on the imports of raw materials.

Little regularity in our series will be found through the cycle of the late twenties and the first half of the thirties. In times of prosperity, foreign demand for American foodstuffs and raw materials lagged behind the general level of demand for American exports. During the Great Depression, a relatively high supply of raw materials and a relatively low supply of foodstuffs appear to have been dominant. Supply conditions maintained their importance through the late thirties in exports of raw materials and crude foodstuffs, but the signs were interchanged as compared with the preceding five years.

The effect of the Second World War on primary product markets also meets our expectations. In both raw materials and crude foodstuffs an important loss of foreign markets for American producers is apparent. On the other hand, the wartime demand of this country for foreign crude foodstuffs was at a relatively high level.

[49]

The Relative Resource Requirements of American Foreign Trade

We finally come to the key concept of our statistical analysis: the relative resource requirements of foreign trade. Study of the shares of resource products in American exports and imports is certainly interesting, but it does not show very precisely the *true* resource requirements of foreign trade. It may indicate the direction in which the true resource requirements were changing, but unless we know approximately what the resource input into an average dollar's worth of natural resource products was, and unless we have some idea about the indirect inputs of resource products in manufactured commodities, the foregoing sections of the present chapter throw very little light on the actual problem.

In Chapter 7 we shall deal in more detail with the gross output requirements of American foreign trade, and in Chapter 9 we shall examine more critically what can actually be inferred concerning the *true* resource requirements. But the first step, that of eliminating some of the difficulties just mentioned, logically belongs in this chapter.

Clearly, if resource requirements per dollar of exports and imports of resource products were roughly similar, and if the resource requirements of products other than resource products were small, then both (1) the ratio of the value of resource products exported to the value of resource products imported and (2) a similar ratio comparing resource product requirements per dollar of exports and imports could serve to approximate satisfactorily the true index of relative resource requirements of foreign trade. We have reproduced these two indexes, again for the selected periods, in Figure 5.7. We refer to the series defined by (1) as relative resource requirements, and to the series defined by (2) as relative resource requirements per dollar. The former series will be more closely analyzed and used in the argument of Chapter 9.

A continuously declining trend is apparent in both indexes. The decline was comparatively smooth during the first four decades of our study. This smoothness can be accounted for not only by the greater economic stability of the period, but also by the ten-year averages which we have recorded here. Two major wars and the Great Depression had a disturbing effect, yet they do not seem to have affected the direction of the trend seriously. The different levels of the two series are due to a persistent surplus of the American trade balance over the 85 years.

Complementary and Supplementary Imports of Resource Products

Customarily we make a distinction between imported commodities which are not produced and those which are produced by the importing

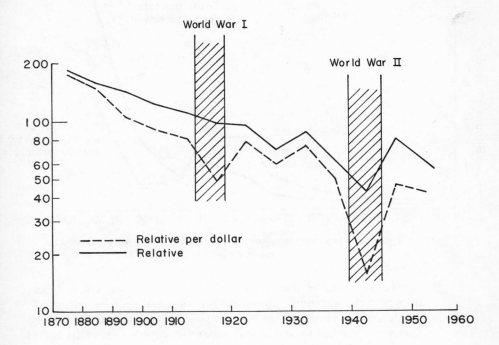

Figure 5.7. United States natural resource requirements of foreign trade, exports divided by imports. *(For sources, see appendix to this chapter.)*

country. We call them complementary and supplementary goods, respectively. In the United States, typical commodities falling within the first group are silk, coffee, and tin, while some falling within the second are petroleum, cotton, and tobacco.

It is the purpose of the present section to trace through the past 85 years these two components of American imports of natural resource products. Actually, the predominant part of American complementary imports are natural resource products. This can be easily explained: Among all factors of production, natural resources are the most inflexible. An American worker can learn within a few years to produce a Swiss watch — but it would be extremely costly, say, to produce natural rubber on Midwestern land.

We have approximated the value of American imports of complementary resource products by totaling leading commodities that represent

[51]

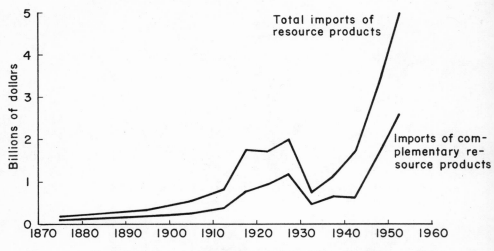

Figure 5.8.   Imports of complementary and supplementary resource products.
(For sources, see appendix to this chapter.)

around 95% of the true values. They are coffee, tea, cocoa beans, tropical fruits and nuts, natural rubber, silk, and tin (ore and metal). This choice of products was forced upon us by statistical availability. Spices and jute had to be omitted, since series covering the entire period were not available. For similar reasons we used aggregate values for tin and tin ore, and omitted certain insignificant imports of ferroalloying metals. Nevertheless, the estimates presented are more than satisfactory for our purpose.

In Figure 5.8 we compare the total with the complementary imports of natural resource products since 1870. The first thing which strikes us is the comparative stability of the two shares. Both complementary and competitive imports of resource products were very close to 50% of the total until 1915. In the period of the First World War, the share of competitive products increased to 60%, with an abnormally high level of imports of wool, hides, and skins. On the other hand, imports of less essential goods, such as coffee and tropical fruits, lagged behind the general level. Again, a similarity will be found between this period and that of the Second World War, during which the share of complementary goods fell as low as 36%. The two decades between wars are marked by a higher proportion of complementary products, approximately 57%. In the postwar decade, we again observe for both groups the 50% share which prevailed during the first four and a half decades of the period under consideration. The fall from 57 to 50% should be imputed mainly to the wartime development of synthetics, especially rubber and fibers (see also Figure 5.4).

It may be interesting to note that the United States appears to be considerably more dependent on complementary foreign supplies of renewable resource products than on mineral resource products. The former always account for around 90% of the values in Figure 5.8. The explanation seems quite straightforward: namely, the random distribution of mineral resources throughout the world as opposed to the systematic character of the American climate.

Regional Distribution of American Foreign Trade in Natural Resource Products

To complete our general survey of American exports and imports of natural resource products, we shall briefly examine the regional distribution of these transactions. Unfortunately we were unable to find data for the entire period examined; however, the available statistics, covering the period from 1905 through World War II, reveal some interesting and meaningful trends.

In Tables 5.2 and 5.3 we show for this period the exports and imports of raw materials, crude foodstuffs, and semi-manufactures, and the percentages, within each commodity class, for different regions: namely, North America, South America, Europe, Asia, Oceania, and Africa.

The impact of different rates of development and industrialization and of some other important factors in the different parts of the world can clearly be distinguished. While imports of raw materials and crude foodstuffs remained fairly stable in relation to this country's total imports, and semi-manufactures increased slightly, this country was gradually shifting to different import sources in the course of the period. Without exception, Europe drastically lost its position in all three commodity classes; its share dropped from 39 to 14% for raw materials, 14 to 4% for crude foodstuffs, and 63 to 36% for semi-manufactures between 1905–10 and 1935–40. (We do not take into account the period of World War II, which reflects the war situation rather than a long-run trend.) Roughly speaking, all other regions with the exception of raw-material imports from North America (mainly Canada) gained from these European losses. Canada as well as many parts of Europe which used to supply this country with primary products and semi-manufactures were undergoing rapid industrialization, and thus absorbed more of their domestic foodstuffs and materials. Primarily because of the rapidly

[53]

growing American demand for silk and natural rubber in the period between wars, Asia and Oceania greatly increased raw-material and semi-manufacture exports to this country.

Europe's position in American exports of resource products is quite similar to that just treated for this country's imports of resource commodities. It was not only the share of European exports to this country but also Europe's imports from the United States that declined in the course of the 40 years. Clearly, relative to total American exports, these declines were even more important than for imports, because of the over-all drop in the share of resource products in American exports. The share of American exports to South America, in all three commodity classes, was unimportant and quite stable. In North America on the other hand, new markets for United States resource products were developed, thus compensating for relative losses incurred in Europe. Most of Asia's increased shares in the classes of raw materials and semi-manufactured goods may be accounted for by American cotton exports.

We may now summarize the evidence presented in this section by pointing out the most important factors. The experience of foreign trade in resource commodities during the first half of this century seems to indicate that regions experiencing a rapid rate of industrial development, such as the United States, Europe, and to some extent Canada, were gradually reducing their mutual dependence on each other's natural resources, turning to other sources in less developed areas where the pressure of domestic demand on natural resources was not so strong. It should be noted, however, that during the period examined (1905–40) the position of Europe as the chief trading partner of this country was becoming less dominant not only in resource products but also in manufactures; it seems that this trend was reversed again after World War II.

In terms of the traditional theory of international trade the developments of the first four decades of this century support the expectation that there will be less basis for trade between regions which develop in the direction of comparable production possibilities. On the other hand, an increasing gap between the levels of development between two regions can only enhance international trading. The reversal of these trends between the years before and the years after World War II reflects to some extent the early stages of industrialization in many underdeveloped parts of the world. But relatively more trading between industrialized countries, and *ipso facto* relatively less trading between the developed and underdeveloped areas, should be accounted for by other factors. Economies of scale leading to international division of

United States Exports by Trading Regions and Commodity Classes, 1906–1945
(values in millions of dollars and percentages)

Description of Statistics	1906–10	1911–15	1921–25	1926–30	1931–35	1936–40	1941–45
Total U.S. exports							
Value (millions of dollars)	1,750	2,331	4,310	4,687	3,166	9,922	1,167
Raw materials exported							
Value (millions of dollars)	554	716	1,187	1,143	601	603	573
Percentage of total value	31.5	30.6	27.5	24.4	30.2	19.05	5.78
Percentage of total raw materials exported to: N. America	10.6	12.1	14.0	15.4	15.8	22.4	45.3
S. America	0.1	0.4	0.7	0.6	0.6	1.5	2.1
Europe	85.8	83.4	73.5	67.6	58.6	56.1	46.2
Asia	} 3.2	} 3.8	} 11.3	} 15.9	} 24.6	} 9.4	} 5.9
Oceania							
Africa	0.3	0.3	0.5	0.5	0.4	0.6	1.5
Crude foodstuffs exported							
Value (millions of dollars)	155	205	420	299	76	119	165
Percentage of total value	8.8	8.8	9.7	6.4	3.8	3.77	1.67
Percentage of total crude foodstuffs exported to: N. America	13.4	24.8	30.4	38.5	28.1	35.5	47.8
S. America	0.1	1.0	1.0	2.6	5.6	2.1	1.0
Europe	83.4	71.0	65.3	54.8	58.4	59.0	41.8
Asia	} 1.8	} 2.4	} 3.3	3.7	7.5	2.8	1.5
Oceania				0.2	0.2	0.2	0.5
Africa	1.3	0.8	0.0	0.2	0.2	0.4	7.4
Semi-manufactures exported							
Value (millions of dollars)	249	359	536	662	288	610	931
Percentage of total value	14.2	15.4	12.4	14.1	14.5	19.3	9.4
Percentage of total semi-manufactures exported to: N. America	15.1	20.6	22.9	24.4	23.0	19.5	26.2
S. America	4.8	5.4	8.6	9.9	7.7	8.2	9.9
Europe	73.4	67.3	49.3	49.3	46.6	44.2	50.7
Asia	} 6.0	} 5.0	} 18.1	} 15.2	} 20.9	23.3	5.2
Oceania						1.9	3.7
Africa	0.7	0.7	1.1	1.2	1.8	2.9	4.3

[55]

TABLE 5.3

United States Imports by Trading Regions and Commodity Classes, 1906–1945
(values in millions of dollars and percentages)

Description of Statistics	1906–10	1911–15	1921–25	1926–30	1931–35	1936–40	1941–45
Total U.S. imports							
Value (millions of dollars)	1,344	1,712	3,450	4,033	1,704	3,440	3,475
Raw materials imported							
Value (millions of dollars)	464	597	290	484	492	807	1,147
Percentage of total value	34.6	34.9	37.4	36.8	28.9	33.1	33.0
Percentage of total raw materials imported from:							
N. America	17.9	19.2	15.9	12.1	10.7	10.1	17.3
S. America	13.4	13.3	10.2	11.5	13.3	14.8	27.0
Europe	38.9	38.5	19.6	17.3	19.2	13.5	4.9
Asia ⎱ Oceania	26.4	25.4	50.7	55.9	53.8	56.1	38.1
Africa	3.4	3.6	3.6	3.2	3.0	5.5	12.7
Crude foodstuffs imported							
Value (millions of dollars)	147	219	382	506	265	319	568
Percentage of total value	1.0	12.8	11.1	12.6	15.6	13.1	16.4
Percentage of total crude foodstuffs imported from:							
N. America	23.8	26.4	29.5	28.6	28.7	33.9	45.8
S. America	49.8	47.1	51.6	53.7	53.5	45.4	41.7
Europe	14.4	14.9	7.2	6.7	5.9	3.5	1.4
Asia	14.0	11.4	8.9	7.5	8.2	10.5	7.2
Oceania	0.0			—	0.0	—	0.2
Africa	0.0	0.2	2.8	3.5	3.7	6.7	3.7
Semi-manufactures imported							
Value (millions of dollars)	239	297	609	762	319	510	735
Percentage of total value	17.3	17.4	17.7	18.9	18.7	20.9	21.2
Percentage of total semi-manufactures imported from:							
N. America	18.2	15.1	23.5	24.2	24.4	25.7	51.7
S. America	7.7	8.7	12.9	11.1	3.1	9.3	24.6
Europe	63.4	54.0	43.5	42.6	44.0	35.6	4.0
Asia	10.7	12.1	17.9	18.9	21.7	27.5	9.9
Oceania						0.0	0.8
Africa		0.1	3.3	3.2	1.8	1.9	6.0

labor as well as many institutional and policy factors, like tariff reductions and customs unions, have certainly contributed to this reversal.

Statistical Appendix to Chapter 5

Note on Tables 5.4 through 5.8

The bulk of the information presented in these tables has been compiled from the foreign trade section of the *Statistical Abstract of the United States.*[9] For certain periods we have computed the five-year averages. Others were already available. Unit-value, value, and quantity indexes were available for the period 1913–55 only. We have estimated those for 1870–1913. More will be said about this estimation below.

The trade data concern exports of United States produce and imports for United States consumption; both are valued f.o.b. In 1915 the official United States statistics of foreign trade switched from fiscal (ending June 30) to calendar years. Since we deal mostly with ten-year averages in this period, we believe that no important bias can have arisen from this change of definition, and therefore no adjustment has been made.

The unit-value indexes for economic classes following 1913 are chained indexes computed by the Fisher method, using the preceding year as the base in the calculations for each year. In each class, index numbers are based on a representative sample of commodities. It was not possible to establish the coverage. Using these, quantity indexes were directly derived from corresponding value relatives.

Unit-Value and Quantity Indexes, 1870–1913

Estimates were made for total trade, raw materials, and crude foodstuffs only, since we are primarily interested in the first two commodity classes (resource products).

Total export and import unit-value indexes for the relevant periods were derived from "Export and Import Prices in the United States and the Terms of International Trade, 1880–1914," *Quarterly Journal of Economics,* 1926, p. 708. Only the last two years were available for the first decade, 1871–80. Simple averages were calculated from these index numbers for the three and a half decades, and they were linked to the latter series up through 1913. Value relatives for total trade were calculated from available value data, and the quantity indexes were derived by simple division.

[9] U.S. Dept. of Commerce, Bureau of the Census, *Statistical Abstract of the United States* (Washington, D.C., Government Printing Office, published annually).

Unit values for exports and imports of raw materials and crude foodstuffs were estimated as a weighted average of price data for representative commodities of the corresponding classes. Average values of these commodities traded during the period were used as weights. For exports and imports of crude foodstuffs, the estimation was particularly simple, since wheat in the first class and coffee in the second covered well over 60% of their respective totals during the period considered. For exports of raw materials we have based our index on coal, cotton, and tobacco, which cover nearly 100% of the total of the class. Prices of wool, silk, and rubber were used for estimation of the unit-value index for imports of raw materials. Here the coverage is quite low, never exceeding 40%.

The price series for the different commodities entering these indexes were taken mainly from the *Statistical Abstract of the United States*, from *Agricultural Statistics*,[10] and from a study by J. Pedersen and O. S. Petersen, *An Analysis of Price Behavior during the Period 1850–1913*.[11]

Value relatives were again obtained from total-value data and quantity indexes from these and the unit-value indexes estimated.

[10] U.S. Dept. of Agriculture, *Agricultural Statistics* (Washington, D.C., Government Printing Office, published annually).

[11] J. Pedersen and O. S. Petersen, *An Analysis of Price Behavior during the Period 1850–1913* (Copenhagen, Levin & Munksgaard, 1938).

TABLE 5.4

United States Foreign Trade
Class 1: Raw Materials
(yearly averages)

Period Ending (5 or 10 years)	Quantity	Unit Value	Value	Value (millions of dollars)	Value (percentage of total trade)
		(1923–25 = 100)			
Exports					
1955	121	124	150	1976	13
1950	119	104	124	1629	14
1945	63	69	43	573	6
1940	90	50	45	603	19
1935	105	43	46	601	30
1930	123	70	87	1144	24
1925	99	91	90	1187	28
1920	n.a.*	n.a.	88	1169	18
1915	122	44	54	717	31
1910	90	41	37	493	31
1900	76	29	22	296	30
1890	49	41	20	269	36
1880	33	49	16	216	39
Imports					
1955	153	126	192	2835	26
1950	142	95	135	1992	31
1945	110	71	78	1147	33
1940	107	51	55	807	33
1935	92	36	33	493	29
1930	116	87	101	1484	37
1925	97	90	88	1290	37
1920	n.a.	n.a.	93	1348	40
1915	59	69	41	598	35
1910	41	60	27	395	34
1900	22	64	14	202	26
1890	11	88	10	148	21
1880	6	102	6	92	17

* n.a. = not available.

TABLE 5.5

United States Foreign Trade
Class 2: Crude Foodstuffs
(yearly averages)

Period Ending (5 or 10 years)	Quantity	Unit Value	Value	Value (millions of dollars)	Value (percentage of total trade)
		(1923–25 = 100)			
Exports					
1955	281	119	335	1080	7
1950	235	128	302	972	9
1945	59	86	51	165	2
1940	69	54	37	119	4
1935	46	52	24	77	4
1930	101	92	93	300	6
1925	134	97	130	420	10
1920	n.a.	n.a.	183	588	9
1915	89	72	64	205	9
1910	79	66	52	165	11
1900	104	55	57	183	18
1890	59	71	42	136	18
1880	39	92	36	117	20
Imports					
1955	156	317	494	2105	20
1950	147	196	290	1237	18
1945	152	88	133	569	16
1940	133	56	75	320	13
1935	110	56	62	266	16
1930	109	109	118	507	13
1925	98	81	89	383	11
1920	n.a.	n.a.	95	408	15
1915	64	79	51	219	13
1910	64	50	32	137	12
1900	32	94	30	129	17
1890	30	83	25	106	15
1880	19	108	20	85	16

TABLE 5.6

United States Foreign Trade
Class 3: Manufactured Foodstuffs
(yearly averages)

Period Ending (5 or 10 years)	Quantity	Unit Value	Value	Value (millions of dollars)	Value (percentage of total trade)
		(1923–25 = 100)			
Exports					
1955	102	132	135	775	5
1950	142	139	201	1161	10
1945	182	110	200	1154	12
1940	43	70	30	175	6
1935	49	62	30	177	9
1930	81	97	79	456	10
1925	105	99	104	601	14
1920	n.a.	n.a.	196	1133	18
1915	n.a.	n.a.	58	334	14
(year 1913)	73	76	56		
1910	n.a.	n.a.	55	317	20
1900	,,	,,	44	256	26
1890	,,	,,	33	189	25
1880	,,	,,	22	129	22
Imports					
1955	204	113	231	1088	10
1950	145	102	149	705	11
1945	127	67	85	400	12
1940	149	49	73	346	14
1935	112	44	49	234	14
1930	119	68	80	398	10
1925	96	94	91	448	13
1920	n.a.	n.a.	111	545	16
1915	n.a.	n.a.	44	215	13
(year 1913)	74	54	40		
1910	n.a.	n.a.	28	139	12
1900	,,	,,	26	129	17
1890	,,	,,	25	123	18
1880	,,	,,	23	111	21

TABLE 5.7

United States Foreign Trade
Class 4: Semi-Manufactures
(yearly averages)

Period Ending (5 or 10 years)	Quantity	Unit Value	Value	Value (millions of dollars)	Value (percentage of total trade)
		(1923–25 = 100)			
Exports					
1955	173	167	288	1765	12
1950	157	135	212	1295	11
1945	153	100	153	931	9
1940	127	80	101	611	19
1935	72	65	47	289	15
1930	114	95	108	663	14
1925	88	100	88	537	12
1920	n.a.	n.a.	162	987	15
1915	n.a.	n.a.	64	359	15
(year 1913)	91	72	65		
1910	n.a.	n.a.	34	205	13
1900	,,	,,	13	82	8
1890	,,	,,	6	39	5
1880	,,	,,	4	26	5
Imports					
1955	212	171	362	2557	24
1950	153	135	208	1469	22
1945	115	90	104	735	21
1940	101	72	72	511	21
1935	73	62	45	319	19
1930	112	96	107	762	19
1925	87	98	86	609	18
1920	n.a.	n.a.	81	575	17
1915	n.a.	n.a.	42	297	17
(year 1913)	64	75	48		
1910	n.a.	n.a.	28	201	17
1900	,,	,,	15	106	14
1890	,,	,,	15	103	15
1880	,,	,,	10	20	13

TABLE 5.8

United States Foreign Trade
Class 5: Finished Manufactures
(yearly averages)

Period Ending (5 or 10 years)	Quantity	Unit Value	Value	Value (millions of dollars)	Value (percentage of total trade)
		(1923–25 = 100)			
Exports					
1955	434	135	568	9590	63
1950	334	121	404	6612	57
1945	424	102	434	7098	70
1940	148	68	101	1658	52
1935	81	64	52	847	43
1930	143	91	130	2126	45
1925	90	107	96	1566	36
1920	n.a.	n.a.	156	2540	40
1915	n.a.	n.a.	44	716	31
(year 1913)	65	73	48		
1910	n.a.	n.a.	25	409	26
1900	,,	,,	12	189	18
1890	,,	,,	7	117	16
1880	,,	,,	5	87	15
Imports					
1955	177	163	289	2195	20
1950	112	138	155	1177	18
1945	98	84	82	624	18
1940	102	59	60	457	19
1935	89	58	51	393	23
1930	123	93	114	882	22
1925	93	100	93	720	21
1920	n.a.	n.a.	63	484	15
1915	n.a.	n.a.	50	383	23
(year 1913)	84	64	54		
1910	n.a.	n.a.	37	287	25
1900	,,	,,	25	197	27
1890	,,	,,	28	213	31
1880	,,	,,	23	177	33

TABLE 5.9

United States·Foreign Trade
Total Trade
(yearly averages)

Period Ending (5 or 10 years)	Quantity	Unit Value	Value	Value (millions of dollars)
		(1923–25 = 100)		
		Exports		
1955	248	137	340	15189
1950	213	122	261	11672
1945	229	97	222	9922
1940	106	67	71	3167
1935	76	59	45	1989
1930	122	86	105	4688
1925	97	99	96	4310
1920	n.a.	n.a.	142	6417
1915	81	64	52	2332
1910	61	57	35	1589
1900	52	44	23	1006
1890	29	58	17	750
1880	22	60	13	575
		Imports		
1955	153	126	192	10783
1950	140	122	172	6581
1945	117	77	91	3476
1940	113	56	64	2440
1935	92	48	45	1704
1930	116	90	104	4033
1925	94	94	89	3450
1920	n.a.	n.a.	87	3358
1915	64	69	44	1712
1910	48	62	30	1159
1900	32	62	20	763
1890	25	73	18	692
1880	16	86	14	535

TABLE 5.10

Changing Structure of Resource Product Imports to the United States:
Selected Periods, 1871–1955

Period	Coffee	Fruits and Nuts	Hides and Skins	Raw Wool	Crude Rubber	Silk	Crude Petroleum	Iron Ore	Tin and Tin Ore	Total
					(values in millions of current dollars)					
1951–1955	1415	151	75	275	494	29	497	107	218	3261
1936–1940	138	60	51	61	206	109	24	6	85	740
1926–1930	282	85	118	79	294	368	79	0	89	1394
1911–1915	109	43	103	43	83	80	8	0	41	510
1891–1900	83	19	32	22	21	26	0	0	9	212
1871–1880	49	11	7	13	6	6	0	0	3	95
					(percentage of total)					
1951–1955	43.2	4.7	2.3	8.4	15.2	0.9	15.3	3.3	6.7	100
1936–1940	18.7	8.1	6.9	8.3	27.8	14.7	3.2	0.8	11.5	100
1926–1930	20.2	6.1	8.5	5.7	21.1	26.4	5.7	0	6.3	100
1911–1915	21.3	8.4	20.3	8.5	16.0	15.7	1.7	0	8.1	100
1891–1900	39.2	9.0	15.0	10.4	9.9	12.3	0	0	4.2	100
1871–1880	51.7	11.5	7.3	13.7	6.3	6.3	0	0	3.2	100

SOURCE: *Statistical Abstract of the United States, op. cit.*

TABLE 5.11

The Relative Resource Requirements of United States Trade
(yearly averages)

Period	Value of Resource Products				$\frac{100 \times (1)}{(2)}$	$\frac{100 \times (3)}{(4)}$
	Exported (millions of dollars) (1)	Imported (2)	Exported (percentage of total exports) (3)	Imported (percentage of total imports) (4)		
1951–1955	3056	4940	20	46	62	43
1946–1950	2601	3229	23	49	81	47
1941–1945	738	1716	8	49	43	16
1936–1940	722	1127	23	46	64	50
1931–1935	678	759	34	45	89	75
1926–1930	1444	1991	30	50	72	60
1921–1925	1607	1673	38	48	96	79
1916–1920	1737	1756	27	65	99	49
1911–1915	923	817	40	48	113	83
1901–1910	658	532	42	46	123	91
1891–1900	479	331	48	43	145	106
1881–1890	405	254	54	36	160	150
1871–1880	333	177	59	33	189	179

SOURCE: *Statistical Abstract of the United States, op. cit.*

TABLE 6.1

United States Resource Products, Production in Millions of Dollars, Valued at Average Prices of 1935–39, and Apparent Consumption as Percentage of Total Domestic Production

Year	All Resource Products	Agricultural Materials			Fishery and Wildlife Products	Forest Products	Minerals			
		Total	Foods	Non-foods			Total	Metallic Ores	Mineral Fuels	Other Minerals
	Production (millions of dollars)									
1900	8,620	6,259	4,829	1,430	107	1,258	996	189	699	108
1910	10,481	7,131	5,529	1,602	113	1,347	1,890	327	1,356	207
1920	12,133	8,278	6,416	1,862	102	1,161	2,592	399	1,941	252
1930	13,070	8,825	7,270	1,555	145	994	3,106	387	2,308	411
1940	14,793	9,920	8,082	1,838	149	957	3,767	507	2,763	497
1950	18,689	12,190	10,050	2,140	157	1,100	5,242	572	3,788	882
1952	20,284	13,200	10,630	2,570	145	1,139	5,800	628	4,144	1,028
	Apparent Consumption (percentage of production)									
1900	90.8	87.9	93.4	69.3	115.9	97.9	97.5	101.0	93.8	114.8
1910	98.1	97.4	101.2	84.1	120.3	98.8	98.5	104.3	94.7	114.5
1920	98.3	96.6	96.8	95.9	132.4	101.4	100.9	115.8	97.1	106.3
1930	100.7	100.6	102.1	93.6	142.1	102.1	98.5	105.9	96.2	104.9
1940	105.1	105.1	103.9	110.3	157.0	103.5	103.3	139.4	96.8	102.6
1950	104.8	100.6	100.4	101.2	163.7	110.2	111.7	173.8	104.1	103.7
1952	103.7	99.6	98.9	102.6	163.4	109.0	110.3	170.7	102.7	103.9

SOURCE: *Statistical Abstract of the United States*, 1956, p. 731, Table 906.

Some have already been discussed in the preceding chapters. In the course of the first half of this century, over-all real output of resource products in the United States increased by almost 140%, while consumption of these products rose by 170%. Owing to the nature of the demand for such commodities, both of these increases lag considerably behind the real growth of the GNP. The difference between the increases of consumption and output is explained by the net balance of exports and imports. On the whole, our dependence on foreign supplies of resource products was never quantitatively important. In 1940, when it was at its highest, apparent consumption stood only 5% above domestic output and remained at about that level thereafter. This apparently satisfactory picture of the whole, however, conceals much more pronounced trends and absolute scarcities in particular sectors. It should also be remembered that the quantitative dependence on foreign supply is only a poor measure of the contribution of imports to national welfare. The size of such benefits cannot be appraised without knowing how much it would cost to produce substitutes for resource imports domestically. In the case of tropical fruits and metallic minerals, such costs could be extremely high.

In primary foods — the most important single component of the aggregate — the United States experienced throughout the period a remarkable state of balance. This certainly does not mean that there was no trade in this type of commodity, but rather that exports of primary foodstuffs were just about matched by imports. Over the years imports of agricultural materials (non-foods) caught up with our exports. In 1900, the United States was exporting 30% (net) of its output of agricultural materials, while in 1952 output fell short of domestic consumption by 3%.

The two primary producing sectors in which we most strongly depend on foreign supplies, and in which we encounter a rapidly increasing deficiency of domestic output, are fisheries and metallic ores. Of the two sectors, the second is by far the more important. Although output and consumption of metallic ores were nearly balanced in 1900, today consumption exceeds output by more than 70%. Because of a general tendency to replace wood with newly developed materials, wood consumption in recent years is at approximately the same level as it was in 1900. Nevertheless, even in this sector we have failed to increase our output, and thus we have moved from a position of net exporter to that of net importer.

The nature of demand for energy in a growing industrial economy explains the rapid increase of both output and consumption of mineral

fuels. Their consumption has increased by about 500% during the first half of this century, and is today, next to the crude foodstuffs, the second most important consumption sector. But even here, in spite of our over-abundant reserves of coal and crude oil, we have changed from a position of net exporter to net importer. We have experienced an even faster growth in the production of other minerals (i.e, excluding fuels and metallic ores). Surprisingly enough, however, our dependence on foreign supplies here has declined over the years.

To sum up this brief chapter, we may say that, measured in terms of domestic availability, American dependence on foreign supplies of natural resource products was never very important. Nevertheless, the conclusions of the preceding chapter are confirmed by our present findings: Over the past 50 years or so, the United States has moved from the camp of net exporters of natural resource products to that of net importers. A breakdown of total trade and output into their component parts shows that in a number of sectors the United States has been losing its self-sufficiency at a rapid rate.

7

Direct and Indirect Resource Requirements

Measuring the Direct and Indirect Requirements

The preceding two chapters dealt only with the direct requirements of American foreign trade. In other words, we have considered only the resource products traded directly between the United States and the rest of the world. Although the variations observed in the trade structure provide some rough information concerning the resource requirements of our foreign transactions, they do not tell the whole story. A good many resource products flow into and out of this country as input of commodities which have been processed beyond the stage of primary products. The supply of any commodity or service requires a certain amount of resource products.

Clearly, the ideal way of measuring the factor contributions of a given bill of exported or imported goods would be to evaluate the shares contributed by land, capital, and labor. We discussed in Chapter 2 the difficulties involved in such an imputation of values. Besides the virtually insurmountable technical problems, the estimation would be hampered by the conceptual difficulty of imputing factor incomes. In Chapter 2 we also explained our preference for dealing with resource products rather than resource requirements. We have defined these products as all outputs which use extractive resources as a direct input.

It is clear that the productive contribution of land in any given bill of goods must have entered directly or indirectly through resource products. Although we do not know exactly how much rent each resource product contains, we have some information concerning the flow of resource products within our economy. This information is contained in the structural-flow matrix prepared by the Bureau of Labor Statistics for 1947. In this matrix the American economy is subdivided into 192 productive sectors, and for each sector the supplies

72

required per dollar of output of any other sector are recorded. By a calculation shown in greater detail in the appendix to this chapter, it was possible to compute the gross value of resource product requirements per dollar of output for each of the 192 sectors. These coefficients, broken down into replaceable and nonreplaceable resource product requirements, also appear in the appendix to this chapter. The product of the export vector, or of the competitive import vector, and of the resource product requirement vector then yields the resource product requirements of American foreign trade. We have computed (or used available information for) the requirements of each of the 21 resource outputs either for producing our exports or for replacing our competitive imports. We alsq show certain aggregates, such as renewable resource product requirements and nonrenewable resource product requirements.

Although the statistics presented in this chapter provide more reliable information than that offered in the preceding two chapters, several sources of possible bias are still present. As we have mentioned, it is resource *product* requirements and not actual resource requirements that we are computing. This limitation of our statistics was dealt with earlier and thus is passed over here. Moreover, the structural-flow matrix which we had to use for the entire period of 1899–1954 reflects the technical coefficients of the year 1947. Finally, all values recorded in this chapter are valued at 1947 prices. Both of these factors may have some effect on the validity and meaning of our results.

Let us consider first the assumption of constant technology. Clearly, technology has not remained unchanged over the 55-year period which we are considering. The coefficients in the structural-flow matrix were changing with time, and consequently our resource product requirements must also have changed. These changes took place in two directions. On the one hand, input coefficients as a whole were altered from year to year; on the other hand, important technical substitutions took place. From the little information we have, it appears that the general movement was toward lower inputs of materials, i.e., smaller coefficients. This saving of primary products seems to have been most pronounced in industrial fuel consumption. It took about three tons of coking coal to produce a ton of raw iron around the turn of the century; it takes no more than one ton today. Another indication of the reduction of the input coefficients will be found in Leontief's analysis of the structural flows for 1919, 1929, and 1939.

The possible error due to substituting one material for another, however, may be even more troublesome. Substitutions of synthetics for leather, silk, cotton, wool, rubber, etc., which were brought to the reader's

[73]

attention in the earlier chapters, were quite important; the pattern was similar for aluminum, petroleum, and natural gas. Insofar as such substitutions took place between two resource commodities such as bauxite and iron ore, or petroleum and coal, the total resource product requirements may not have been seriously affected because the products were similar. In other cases, however, where a resource product was replaced by a material containing few natural resources, the possible error could have been quite large. This pertains mainly to synthetics.

On the whole, as a result of a growing scarcity of natural resources it seems that both types of changes of technical coefficients saved resource products. The process of substitution often saved resource products, but rarely, if ever, manufactured materials. At the same time, less wasteful uses of materials were found, and new by-products were developed.

The valuation of commodities traded at constant prices may or may not be useful, depending on what answers we wish to obtain from our calculations. The data which we have computed, assuming a constant technology through time, show the physical volumes of the different resource product requirements in different periods of time. Thus, for example, we may find out how much of each particular resource product has flowed on net balance into or out of this country. In a sense, this is a technical, not an economic, fact. The price of a resource product may at one time have been very low or nil, and thus, clearly, no drain or addition to the economic wealth of the United States would have occurred. We have discussed this topic in more detail in Chapter 2.

If values rather than volumes of foreign transactions had been employed, this difficulty might have been avoided. On the whole, however, we may expect that the difference between results obtained in using values would not have been great. As we have seen in Chapter 5, price variations of exported and imported resource products were fairly similar. Over the period considered, unit values of exported raw materials have risen somewhat in comparison with unit values of imported raw materials. An opposite over-all trend may be observed for crude foodstuffs: Our food has become a little less expensive in terms of foreign crude foodstuffs.

Findings

In Tables 7.1a, b, and c we show the direct exports and competitive imports of resource products as well as the gross output (direct and indirect) requirements of these transactions. The selected periods are

TABLE 7.1a

United States Direct Foreign Trade in Natural Resource Products (Dir.), and Its Total Resource Product Requirements (G.O.) for Selected Periods
(millions of dollars, 1947 prices, technology of 1947)

	EXPORTS									
	1899		*1928*		*1937*		*1947*		*1954*	
	Dir.	*G.O.*	*Dir.*	*G.O.*	*Dir.*	*G.O.*	*Dir.*	*G.O.*	*Dir.*	*G.O.*
Renewable Resources:	1757.3	3935.3	2323.9	3346.4	1768.6	2508.0	1707.0	4092.3	1925.2	3301.3
Meat, dairy, etc.	147.6	828.2	155.0	303.1	99.4	169.3	53.0	661.9	51.6	426.3
1. Meat and products	128.8	744.4	83.8	200.1	59.5	109.5	13.7	416.0	15.3	314.6
2. Poultry, eggs	3.5	29.1	14.8	21.4	2.4	6.7	21.3	47.1	22.7	39.2
3. Farm dairy products	—	33.0	3.4	20.5	1.0	8.4	1.2	163.9	0.4	46.8
10. Fisheries, etc.	15.3	21.6	53.0	61.1	36.5	44.7	16.8	34.9	13.2	25.6
Food and grain crops	687.4	1562.2	417.2	727.3	224.3	434.8	1131.7	2150.7	838.4	1411.4
4. Food grains, feed crops	660.2	1450.4	333.0	592.0	144.8	286.6	925.9	1769.3	563.0	917.3
7. Oil-bearing crops	—	58.5	0.2	38.6	3.5	32.7	44.5	149.0	168.4	351.6
8. Vegetables and fruits	27.2	53.3	84.0	96.7	76.0	115.5	161.3	232.4	107.0	142.5
All other renewable resources	922.3	1544.9	9751.7	2316.0	1444.9	1903.9	522.3	1279.7	1035.2	1463.6
5. Cotton	790.4	1187.9	1392.0	1735.3	1179.9	1464.4	393.7	773.6	780.5	1004.6
6. Tobacco	96.1	126.6	313.0	323.1	233.0	239.5	88.2	190.4	215.6	225.2
9. Other agricultural products	35.8	197.8	26.5	182.7	17.6	136.4	34.1	222.2	29.8	164.1
36. Logging	—	32.7	20.2	74.9	14.4	63.6	6.3	93.5	9.3	69.7
Nonrenewable Mineral Resources:	49.2	398.6	233.1	1057.8	380.3	1068.1	531.6	1619.5	181.5	882.5
Metallic minerals	3.0	69.6	56.1	295.3	49.1	253.7	17.0	254.9	20.7	205.5
11. Iron ore mining	0.1	7.0	6.3	31.2	4.6	57.8	9.2	75.5	12.8	47.1
12. Copper mining	0.9	46.1	0.7	149.3	1.7	88.1	—	72.6	0.9	76.3
13. Lead and zinc mining	1.3	5.8	0.6	27.2	—	18.1	0.2	40.9	—	24.5
14. Bauxite mining	—	0.8	6.7	8.9	6.5	8.6	1.9	7.7	0.3	3.5
15. Other metallic mining	0.7	9.7	41.8	78.7	36.3	81.1	5.7	58.2	6.7	44.2
Fuel minerals	41.1	302.0	152.4	700.8	302.0	746.5	471.3	1243.6	147.8	645.3
16. Coal mining	41.1	110.1	118.0	218.2	120.0	323.4	367.1	596.5	144.8	273.5
17. Crude petroleum and natural gas	—	191.8	34.4	482.6	182.0	514.1	104.2	647.1	3.0	351.9
Nonmetallic, non-fuel minerals	5.1	27.1	24.6	61.7	29.2	67.9	43.3	116.0	13.0	61.6
18. Sand, stone, clay, etc.	5.1	15.2	5.3	21.2	5.3	22.9	5.5	36.6	1.0	21.5
19. Sulphur	—	3.5	19.3	25.2	23.8	29.6	23.1	35.1	2.4	10.4
20. Other nonmetallic	—	8.4	—	15.3	0.1	15.4	14.7	44.3	9.6	29.7
TOTAL RESOURCES	1806.5	4334.0	2557.0	4404.2	2148.9	3576.1	2238.6	5706.8	2106.7	4183.7

TABLE 7.1b

United States Direct Foreign Trade in Natural Resource Products (Dir.),
and Its Total Resource Product Requirements (G.O.) for Selected Periods
(millions of dollars, 1947 prices, technology of 1947)

| | *COMPETITIVE IMPORTS* | | | | | | | | | |
| | *1899* | | *1928* | | *1937* | | *1947* | | *1954* | |
	Dir.	*G.O.*	*Dir.*	*G.O.*	*Dir.*	*G.O.*	*Dir.*	*G.O.*	*Dir.*	*G.O.*
Renewable Resources:	**364.9**	**1433.1**	**1302.5**	**2589.0**	**1239.5**	**2464.2**	**1061.5**	**2363.2**	**1045.5**	**2501.3**
Meat, dairy, etc.	*46.3*	*369.6*	*819.0*	*1069.7*	*571.9*	*736.6*	*507.1*	*669.4*	*423.5*	*801.6*
1. Meat and products	30.3	315.1	573.4	797.5	453.0	593.9	338.1	456.0	312.3	627.1
2. Poultry, eggs	1.2	18.9	5.6	10.8	2.2	7.5	4.9	14.5	9.2	26.9
3. Farm dairy products	—	12.7	41.0	54.3	24.8	34.7	—	17.1	—	34.9
10. Fisheries, etc.	14.8	22.8	199.0	207.1	91.9	100.5	164.1	181.8	102.0	112.7
Food and grain crops	*58.0*	*351.1*	*253.6*	*845.9*	*485.2*	*1143.5*	*311.2*	*822.0*	*315.0*	*890.1*
4. Food grains, feed crops	8.5	232.3	60.9	486.8	281.0	665.0	6.8	297.7	107.3	499.3
7. Oil-bearing crops	—	37.6	92.6	224.3	173.2	402.5	159.4	283.8	73.1	177.9
8. Vegetables and fruits	49.5	81.2	100.1	134.8	31.0	76.0	145.0	240.5	134.8	212.9
All other renewable resources	*260.6*	*712.4*	*229.9*	*673.4*	*182.4*	*584.1*	*243.2*	*871.8*	*306.8*	*809.6*
5. Cotton	24.7	139.3	44.4	152.7	34.5	114.7	50.0	98.3	25.5	109.2
6. Tobacco	66.4	87.1	85.0	88.3	53.8	55.5	0.2	61.2	69.3	74.8
9. Other agricultural products	169.5	466.1	86.3	315.8	81.5	291.2	136.5	502.5	138.3	387.8
36. Logging	—	19.9	14.2	116.6	12.6	122.7	56.5	209.8	73.7	237.8
Nonrenewable Mineral Resources:	**47.8**	**158.0**	**286.9**	**673.2**	**201.2**	**586.6**	**702.6**	**1248.3**	**1054.0**	**1864.2**
Metallic minerals	*14.9*	*40.2*	*177.0*	*360.9*	*154.0*	*350.7*	*338.6*	*575.3*	*452.8*	*885.5*
11. Iron ore mining	2.0	5.7	7.1	11.3	6.7	12.2	47.4	56.1	72.3	81.5
12. Copper mining	3.6	15.2	18.4	107.4	8.5	64.8	32.5	122.1	50.7	187.0
13. Lead and zinc mining	6.3	10.8	14.2	39.9	1.6	37.5	33.1	77.1	120.9	197.8
14. Bauxite mining	—	0.4	1.5	3.7	5.2	7.5	23.2	25.9	28.8	31.0
15. Other metallic mining	3.0	8.1	135.8	198.6	132.0	228.7	202.4	293.5	180.1	388.3
Fuel minerals	*16.4*	*85.2*	*95.3*	*275.3*	*41.3*	*186.3*	*232.4*	*507.7*	*423.8*	*767.8*
16. Coal mining	16.4	54.6	7.5	79.4	11.3	73.7	1.6	85.7	1.4	106.7
17. Crude petroleum and natural gas	—	30.6	87.8	195.9	30.0	112.6	230.8	422.0	422.4	661.2
Nonmetallic, non-fuel minerals	*16.5*	*32.5*	*14.6*	*55.0*	*5.9*	*49.6*	*131.6*	*165.3*	*177.4*	*210.9*
18. Sand, stone, clay, etc.	8.6	17.4	10.4	20.8	5.1	15.7	23.8	35.6	52.1	64.5
19. Sulphur	5.7	8.3	1.1	8.9	—	7.9	—	7.5	0.1	9.3
20. Other nonmetallic	2.2	6.9	3.1	25.3	0.8	26.0	107.8	122.2	125.2	137.1
TOTAL RESOURCES	**412.7**	**1591.1**	**1589.4**	**3262.2**	**1440.7**	**3050.8**	**1769.1**	**3611.5**	**2099.5**	**4365.4**

TABLE 7.1c

United States Direct Foreign Trade in Natural Resource Products (Dir.),
and Its Total Resource Product Requirements (G.O.) for Selected Periods
(millions of dollars, 1947 prices, technology of 1947)

	1899		1928		1937		1947		1954	
NET TRADE										
	Dir.	G.O.	Dir.	G.O.	Dir.	G.O.	Dir.	G.O.	Dir.	G.O.
Renewable Resources:	1395.8	2502.2	1021.4	757.4	529.1	43.8	645.5	1729.0	879.7	799.9
Meat, dairy, etc.	101.3	458.7	−664.0	−766.6	−472.5	−567.3	−454.1	−7.5	−371.9	−375.5
1. Meat and products	98.5	429.3	−489.6	−597.4	−393.5	−484.4	−324.4	−39.9	−297.0	−312.6
2. Poultry, eggs	2.3	10.2	9.2	10.6	−0.2	−0.8	16.4	32.4	13.5	12.2
3. Farm dairy products	—	20.3	−37.6	−33.8	−23.8	−26.3	1.2	146.8	0.4	11.9
10. Fisheries, etc.	0.5	−1.1	−146.0	−146.0	−55.4	−55.4	−147.3	−196.8	−88.8	−87.1
Food and grain crops	629.4	1211.0	163.6	−118.6	−260.9	−708.7	820.5	1328.8	523.2	521.4
4. Food grains, feed crops	651.7	1218.1	272.1	105.2	−136.2	−378.4	919.1	1471.7	455.7	418.0
7. Oil-bearing crops	—	20.9	−92.4	−185.7	−169.7	−369.8	−114.9	−134.8	95.3	173.8
8. Vegetables and fruits	−22.3	−27.9	−16.1	−38.1	45.0	39.5	16.3	−8.1	−27.8	−70.5
All other renewable resources	661.7	832.5	1521.8	1642.6	1262.5	1319.8	279.1	407.7	728.4	654.0
5. Cotton	765.7	1048.6	1347.6	1582.6	1145.4	1349.7	343.7	675.2	755.0	895.4
6. Tobacco	29.7	39.5	228.0	234.8	179.2	184.0	88.0	129.2	146.3	150.4
9. Other agricultural products	−133.7	−268.3	−59.8	−133.1	−63.9	−159.8	−102.4	−280.3	−108.5	−223.7
36. Logging	—	12.7	6.0	−31.7	1.8	−59.1	−50.2	−116.4	−64.4	−168.0
Nonrenewable Mineral Resources:	1.4	240.4	−53.8	366.6	179.1	481.5	−171.0	366.1	−872.5	−981.5
Metallic minerals	−11.9	29.3	−120.9	−65.6	−104.9	−97.0	−321.6	−320.4	−432.1	−689.8
11. Iron ore mining	1.9	1.3	−0.8	19.9	−2.1	45.6	−38.2	19.4	−59.5	−34.3
12. Copper mining	−2.7	31.0	−17.7	41.9	−6.8	23.3	−32.5	−49.5	−49.8	−110.7
13. Lead and zinc mining	−5.0	−5.0	−13.6	−12.7	−1.6	−19.4	−32.9	−36.7	−120.9	−173.3
14. Bauxite mining	—	−0.4	5.2	5.2	1.3	1.1	−21.3	−18.3	−28.5	−27.5
15. Other metallic mining	−2.3	1.6	−94.0	−119.9	−95.7	−147.6	−196.7	−235.3	−173.4	−344.0
Fuel minerals	24.7	216.6	57.1	425.5	260.7	560.2	238.9	735.9	−276.0	−142.6
16. Coal mining	24.7	55.4	110.5	138.8	108.7	158.7	365.5	510.8	143.4	166.7
17. Crude petroleum and natural gas	—	161.2	−53.4	286.7	152.0	401.5	−126.6	225.1	−419.4	−309.3
Nonmetallic, non-fuel minerals	−11.4	−5.5	10.0	6.7	23.3	18.3	−88.3	−49.4	−164.4	−149.2
18. Sand, stone, clay, etc.	−3.5	−2.2	−5.1	0.4	0.2	7.2	−18.3	0.9	−51.1	−43.0
19. Sulphur	−5.7	−4.7	18.2	16.3	23.8	21.7	23.1	27.6	2.3	1.1
20. Other nonmetallic	−2.2	1.5	−3.1	−10.0	−0.7	−10.6	−93.1	−77.9	−115.6	−107.3
TOTAL RESOURCES	1393.8	2742.6	967.6	1124.0	708.2	525.3	474.5	2095.1	7.2	−181.6

1899, 1928, 1937, 1947, and 1954. We use the classification of the Bureau of Labor Statistics and show the requirements of industries Nos. 1 through 20 and 36. Also shown in the table are total resource product requirements and renewable and nonrenewable resource requirements, as well as subtotals for meat and dairy products, food and grain crops, other renewable resources, metallic minerals, fuel minerals, and other minerals. In addition to exports and competitive imports, we have calculated the net trade for direct requirements and for gross output. The volumes of *net imports* are shown with a minus sign.[1]

In all other chapters of this study, we deal with visible transactions of foreign trade. Here, however, we evaluate direct and indirect resource product requirements of the exports and imports on current account. Thus, in the figures of Table 7.1 we find not only the resource products contained in, say, automobiles, but also the resource contribution to the services of wholesale trade or ocean shipping. Clearly, this does not change the final results significantly from what they would be if the commercial balance of trade alone were considered, because resource requirements of the service industries are generally very low. For example, the reader can find in Table 7.2 in the appendix to this chapter that the ocean shipping industry requires only 4.1 cents' worth of resource products (of all kinds) per dollar of final output.

Let us consider first the totals. With the exception of 1954, this country has always supplied the rest of the world with more resource commodities of the type produced in the United States (either directly traded or contained in manufactures) than it has received from the rest of the world. Clearly, the balance would be different if both competitive and complementary goods were considered. The latter, however, could not be included in the calculations because we do not produce them domestically and thus their technology is unknown.

Similar to the trends noted in earlier chapters, the over-all decline of net exports of resource products over time will also be found here. In relative terms, considering the ratio of export requirements to import requirements, a milder decline over the 55 years will be observed for the gross output requirements than for the direct requirements. Certainly this results from the fact that with the declining share of resource commodities in total trade, relatively more resource products will be channeled through manufactured goods. In Figure 7.1 we compare two ratios: (1) the direct and (2) the direct and indirect requirements of exports over imports. The only figure in the two series which is out of

[1] For sources and a detailed account of the methods of estimation, see the appendix to this chapter. Minor numerical inconsistences for the first two and the last periods are imputable to rounding and (presumably) to other reasons. The figures were taken without change from the original documents referred to in the appendix.

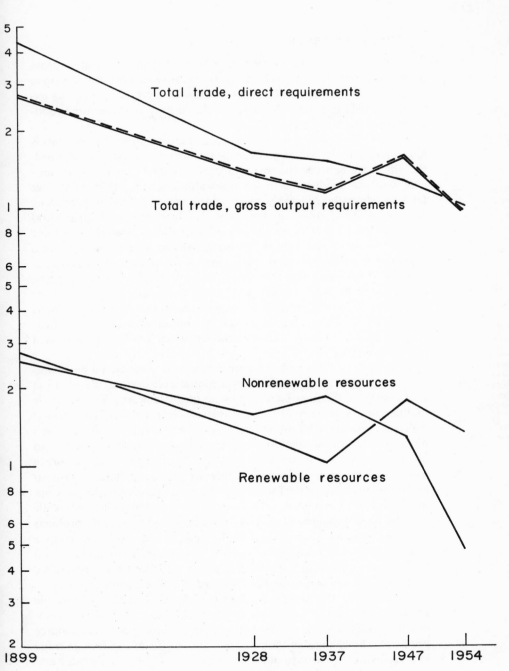

Figure 7.1. Relative gross output requirements of American foreign trade, exports divided by competitive imports: total and economic classes. (*Underlying data computed from Table* 7.1.)

line with the continuous downward trend is that for the relative gross output requirements in 1947. Actually, because of postwar economic assistance, a great amount of indirect resource requirements was exported in 1947 to foreign countries in the form of manufactured foodstuffs and semi-manufactures.

A general comparison between direct and gross output requirements is also interesting. In American exports, throughout the period examined, the difference between the two measures is much larger for nonrenewable resource products than for renewable ones. In other words, we tend to export considerably more added value in further processing with our mineral resources than with our foodstuffs and agricultural raw materials. In 1954, with each dollar of direct renewable resource products we exported only about one dollar and seventy cents of gross output of these commodities, while close to five dollars of gross output of mineral resources was exported with each dollar of direct exports. An opposite pattern will be observed for imports, especially in more recent years. While we tend to import renewable resource products primarily contained in highly fabricated commodities, imports of fuels and minerals are mostly primary products which are further processed in this country.

While the over-all trends for both direct requirements and gross outputs of resource commodities show a comparable decline, the situation with respect to different sectors is by no means uniform. The net trade of different resource product sectors is shown in Table 7.1c. The greatest deficiency will again be found in the metallic minerals sector. It is even more pronounced in relation to the gross output requirements than to direct requirements, as studied in the preceding chapter. Other sectors in which we have been net importers recently are fuel minerals and meat and dairy products. In the former case, however, this is a recent development which was preceded by net exports of coal and petroleum, while our relative dependence on foreign supplies of meat and dairy products has been reduced since the period between world wars. The relative gross output requirements of trade in metallic minerals and mineral fuels are also shown in Figure 7.2, together with those for food grains, meat and dairy products, and all other renewable resource products.

On the whole, the American position in the world trade of renewable resources has been much more erratic with respect to different commodity groups (see Figure 7.2) than was our position in mineral resource products. The changes in the relative requirements of our foreign trade in these two broad groups of natural resource products (renewable and nonrenewable) are shown in Figure 7.1. A temporary disturbance of

[80]

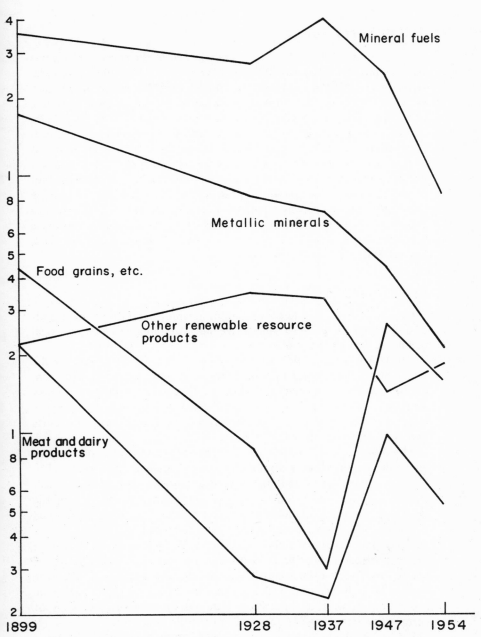

Figure 7.2. Relative gross output requirements of American foreign trade, exports divided by competitive imports: selected economic classes. (*Under-lying data computed from Table 7.1.*)

both series in 1937 and 1947 can be attributed to the special conditions immediately preceding and following World War II. While the mineral resource requirements series shows in the long run a continuous and accelerated trend, the relative requirements of renewable resource products mostly declined between the turn of the century and 1928. In the past 30 years or so, this series seems to have reached a plateau.

As can be seen by examining Figure 7.2, the three relative requirements series underlying the renewable resource requirements of trade (meat, grains, and other renewable resource products) have undergone important irregular changes in the past. Most of this irregularity may be accounted for by postwar reconstruction, income and price elasticities combined with the depressed conditions of the thirties, long-run forces (Chapter 8 is especially devoted to this aspect), and last but not least, United States farm policies.

Appendix to Chapter 7

Chapter 7 was restricted to economic interpretation of an input-output analysis applied to American exports and imports. The statistical technique and its limitations are presented in this appendix.

All data for 1899, 1947, and 1954 were taken from a study by the University of Maryland Bureau of Business and Economic Research, entitled *Some Relationships Between U.S. Consumption and Natural Resources, 1899, 1947, 1954*. We collected similar data to compute direct and indirect resource product requirements of American exports and competitive imports for 1928 and 1937.

The *direct requirements* in Table 7.1 represent exports or imports of the particular commodity or commodity group, valued at 1947 prices. The *gross requirements*, also valued at constant prices, include both direct exports or competitive imports of the item named on the left of the table and all other quantities of the particular commodity contained as inputs in any other commodity or service traded.

Under the Bureau of Labor Statistics classification of the American productive sector into 192 industries, 21 industries using extractive resources as direct input were defined as resource industries. They are Nos. 1 through 20 and No. 36, as listed in Table 7.2 (pp. 84-88). The gross outputs of these industries required for American exports or competitive imports were obtained in the following way:

Let (b_{ij}) be the inverse of $(I - A)$, where I is an identity matrix and A the 192-by-192 (input-output) structural-flow matrix; $\{t_i^x\}$ and $\{t_i^m\}$ are the export and competitive import vectors. Then the gross output of

[82]

a particular resource product R_j ($j = 1, \ldots, 20$ and 36) required for a given set of exports (imports) will be obtained as the inner product of the jth column of (b_{ij}), (B_{ij}), and $\{t_i^x\}$ or $\{t_i^m\}$; i.e.,

$$R_j^x = (B_{ij}) \cdot \{t_i^x\} \qquad j = 1, \ldots, 20, \text{ and } 36$$

and

$$R_j^m = (B_{ij}) \cdot \{t_i^m\} \qquad j = 1, \ldots, 20, \text{ and } 36$$

Summing up the elements of b_{ij} across the columns 1 through 10 and column 36, we obtain the total renewable resource requirements per dollar of final demand (P). Summing up across the columns 11 through 20, we obtain the total requirements of nonrenewable resource products per dollar of final demand of the particular row (N). As an interesting illustration of the importance of the inputs of natural resources in different commodities, we have reproduced below the *resource coefficients* (P and N) for the 192 different industrial sectors. Total resource requirements can be obtained by adding the two columns.

The methods and statistical sources used by the Bureau of Business and Economic Research in estimating the export and import vectors, valued in constant prices, will be found in the document mentioned earlier. As our basic source of foreign trade statistics, we used the detailed trade return as presented in the pre–World War II volumes of the *Statistical Abstract of the United States*. Data for sea transportation were taken from United States balance-of-payments statistics. On the whole, because of limited resources, our estimates are probably inferior to those of the Bureau of Business and Economic Research. The chief definitional difference between the two sets of data is that we had to use f.o.b. export and import figures, whereas the other studies valued traded commodities at factory price and imputed the rest of their value to domestic transportation sectors. This difference in procedure will create a bias in computing natural resource requirements of foreign trade, because resource coefficients of the transportation industries are generally lower than those of an "average industry." But considering the relative importance of the domestic transportation sectors in 1947 and 1954, we may conclude that this bias is negligible. Moreover, we were not able to check item by item the entries included in the different export and import industries in our estimation against those of the Bureau of Labor Statistics and the Bureau of Business and Economic Research.

Finally, we believe that the price and/or unit-value indexes which we have employed in deflating the current values to the level of 1947 are inferior to those used for 1899 and 1954. Our calculations, wherever possible, used a price or unit-value index for the particular entry of the 192-industry classification. Whenever such an index was not available, we assumed that export or import unit values moved parallel to the unit-value index of the Department of Commerce (Bureau of Foreign Commerce), calculated for five important economic classes. In deflating the overseas transportation (Bureau of Labor Statistics, No. 172), we have used a compound freight rate index, taken from Charles P. Kindleberger, *The Terms of Trade: A European Case Study* (New York and Cambridge, Mass., John Wiley & Sons and The Technology Press, 1956), p. 19.

TABLE 7.2

Gross Resource Product Requirements per Dollar of Final Output
of 192 Industries
(in dollars)

Number	Industry	Renewable (P)	Nonrenewable (N)
1.	Meat animals and products	1.663	0.021
2.	Poultry and eggs	1.718	0.028
3.	Farm dairy products	1.470	0.023
4.	Food grains and feed crops	1.134	0.033
5.	Cotton	1.298	0.029
6.	Tobacco	1.031	0.019
7.	Oil-bearing crops	1.168	0.028
8.	Vegetables and fruits	1.077	0.021
9.	All other agricultural products	1.079	0.025
10.	Fisheries, hunting, and trapping	1.032	0.014
11.	Iron ore mining	0.013	1.025
12.	Copper mining	0.012	1.029
13.	Lead and zinc mining	0.015	1.029
14.	Bauxite mining	0.005	1.023
15.	Other metal mining	0.020	1.035
16.	Coal mining	0.017	1.020
17.	Crude petroleum and natural gas	0.001	1.018
18.	Stone, sand, clay, and abrasives	0.004	1.051
19.	Sulphur	0.001	1.012
20.	Other nonmetallic minerals	0.004	1.061
21.	Meat packing and wholesale poultry	1.336	0.021
22.	Processed dairy products	0.906	0.026
23.	Canning, preserving, and freezing	0.431	0.027
24.	Grain mill products	0.611	0.027
25.	Bakery products	0.285	0.021
26.	Miscellaneous food products	0.316	0.022
27.	Sugar	0.402	0.039
28.	Alcoholic beverages	0.198	0.023

Table 7.2 (continued)

Number	Industry	Renewable (P)	Nonrenewable (N)
29.	Tobacco manufactures	0.491	0.017
30.	Spinning, weaving, and dyeing	0.404	0.023
31.	Special textile products	0.248	0.014
32.	Jute, linen, cordage, and twine	0.152	0.011
33.	Canvas products	0.182	0.016
34.	Apparel	0.163	0.012
35.	House furnishing and other non-apparel	0.237	0.021
36.	Logging	1.019	0.029
37.	Sawmills, planing and veneer mills	0.189	0.025
38.	Plywood	0.208	0.019
39.	Fabricated wood products	0.073	0.018
40.	Wood containers and cooperage	0.103	0.021
41.	Wood furniture	0.078	0.021
42.	Metal furniture	0.065	0.034
43.	Partitions, screens, shades, etc.	0.055	0.033
44.	Pulp mills	0.305	0.051
45.	Paper and board mills	0.125	0.052
46.	Converted paper products	0.063	0.037
47.	Printing and publishing	0.026	0.015
48.	Industrial inorganic chemicals	0.017	0.180
49.	Industrial organic chemicals	0.067	0.102
50.	Plastic materials	0.090	0.062
51.	Synthetic rubber	0.039	0.117
52.	Synthetic fiber	0.054	0.050
53.	Explosives and fireworks	0.049	0.050
54.	Drugs and medicines	0.062	0.026
55.	Soap and related products	0.288	0.039
56.	Paints and allied products	0.139	0.114
57.	Gum and wood chemicals	0.388	0.029
58.	Fertilizers	0.030	0.176
59.	Vegetable oils	0.797	0.029
60.	Animal oils	0.746	0.035
61.	Miscellaneous chemical industries	0.118	0.083
62.	Petroleum products	0.005	0.598
63.	Coke and products	0.011	0.508
64.	Paving and roofing materials	0.037	0.149
65.	Tires and inner tubes	0.104	0.062
66.	Miscellaneous rubber products	0.055	0.043
67.	Leather tanning and finishing	0.027	0.013
68.	Other leather products	0.041	0.012
69.	Footwear (excluding rubber)	0.030	0.012
70.	Glass	0.011	0.050
71.	Cement	0.007	0.152
72.	Structural clay products	0.003	0.171
73.	Pottery and related products	0.009	0.062
74.	Concrete and plaster products	0.014	0.128

Table 7.2 (continued)

Number	Industry	Renewable (P)	Nonrenewable (N)
75.	Abrasive products	0.049	0.075
76.	Asbestos products	0.019	0.130
77.	Other nonmetallic minerals	0.006	0.211
78.	Blast furnaces	0.009	0.440
79.	Steel works and rolling mills	0.006	0.175
80.	Iron foundries	0.005	0.065
81.	Steel foundries	0.006	0.099
82.	Primary copper	0.010	0.700
83.	Copper rolling and drawing	0.007	0.366
84.	Primary lead	0.014	0.805
85.	Primary zinc	0.007	0.412
86.	Other primary metals	0.013	0.671
87.	Nonferrous metal rolling	0.007	0.271
88.	Primary aluminum	0.006	0.124
89.	Aluminum rolling and drawing	0.005	0.083
90.	Secondary nonferrous metals	0.003	0.126
91.	Nonferrous foundries	0.004	0.079
92.	Iron and steel foundries	0.004	0.103
93.	Tin cans and other tin ware	0.013	0.100
94.	Cutlery	0.010	0.030
95.	Tools and general hardware	0.007	0.039
96.	Other hardware	0.006	0.047
97.	Metal plumbing and vitreous fixtures	0.009	0.071
98.	Heating equipment	0.007	0.047
99.	Structural metal products	0.005	0.058
100.	Boiler shop products and pipe bending	0.005	0.061
101.	Metal stampings	0.008	0.059
102.	Metal coating and engraving	0.005	0.066
103.	Lighting fixtures	0.010	0.042
104.	Fabricated wire products	0.007	0.116
105.	Metal barrels, drums, etc.	0.007	0.080
106.	Tubes and foils	0.009	0.063
107.	Miscellaneous fabricated metal products	0.005	0.054
108.	Steel springs	0.007	0.074
109.	Nuts, bolts, screw machine products	0.005	0.065
110.	Steam engines and turbines	0.004	0.046
111.	Internal combustion engines	0.005	0.043
112.	Farm and industrial tractors	0.008	0.047
113.	Farm equipment	0.010	0.050
114.	Construction and mining machinery	0.005	0.038
115.	Oil-field machinery and tools	0.005	0.045
116.	Machine tools and metalworking machinery	0.004	0.030
117.	Cutting tools, jigs, and fixtures	0.004	0.025
118.	Special industrial machinery	0.009	0.035
119.	Pumps and compressors	0.005	0.039
120.	Elevators and conveyors	0.005	0.039

Table 7.2 (continued)

Number	Industry	Renewable (P)	Nonrenewable (N)
121.	Blowers and fans	0.005	0.036
122.	Power transmission equipment	0.005	0.038
123.	Other industrial machinery	0.007	0.044
124.	Other commercial machinery and equipment	0.007	0.024
125.	Refrigeration equipment	0.009	0.045
126.	Valves and fittings	0.004	0.052
127.	Ball and roller bearings	0.003	0.035
128.	Machine shops	0.003	0.035
129.	Wiring devices and graphite products	0.011	0.060
130.	Electrical measuring instruments	0.007	0.033
131.	Motors and generators	0.007	0.049
132.	Transformers	0.016	0.069
133.	Electrical control apparatus	0.008	0.040
134.	Electrical welding apparatus	0.018	0.049
135.	Electrical appliances	0.010	0.041
136.	Industrial wire and cable	0.017	0.176
137.	Engine electrical equipment	0.008	0.062
138.	Electrical lamps	0.007	0.032
139.	Radio and related products	0.015	0.030
140.	Tubes	0.005	0.044
141.	Communication equipment	0.009	0.036
142.	Storage batteries	0.029	0.129
143.	Primary batteries	0.007	0.087
144.	X-ray apparatus	0.006	0.021
145.	Motor vehicles	0.021	0.054
146.	Truck trailers	0.031	0.040
147.	Automobile trailers	0.028	0.036
148.	Aircraft and parts	0.006	0.026
149.	Ships and boats	0.012	0.027
150.	Locomotives	0.007	0.046
151.	Railroad equipment	0.010	0.054
152.	Motorcycles and bicycles	0.011	0.034
153.	Instruments, etc.	0.008	0.030
154.	Optical, ophthalmic, and photo equipment	0.014	0.030
155.	Medical and dental instruments and supplies	0.096	0.028
156.	Watches and clocks	0.007	0.030
157.	Jewelry and silverware	0.007	0.116
158.	Musical instruments and parts	0.021	0.018
159.	Toys and sporting goods	0.027	0.027
160.	Office supplies	0.027	0.018
161.	Plastic products	0.055	0.024
162.	Cork products	0.009	0.023
163.	Motion picture products	0.005	0.010
164.	Miscellaneous manufactured products	0.054	0.027

Table 7.2 (continued)

Number	Industry	Renewable (P)	Nonrenewable (N)
165.	} (excluded)		
166.			
167.	Electric light and power	0.003	0.118
168.	Natural, manufactured, and mixed gas	0.001	0.198
169.	Railroads	0.006	0.066
170.	Trucking	0.007	0.036
171.	Warehousing and storage	0.026	0.013
172.	Ocean shipping	0.007	0.034
173.	Other water transportation	0.006	0.084
174.	Air transportation	0.007	0.044
175.	Pipeline transportation	0.001	0.027
176.	Wholesale trade	0.007	0.009
177.	Retail trade	0.005	0.013
178.	Local and highway transportation	0.003	0.031
179.	Telephone and telegraph	0.005	0.003
180.	Eating and drinking places	0.261	0.017
181.	Banking, finance, and insurance	0.003	0.004
182.	Hotels	0.009	0.012
183.	Real estate and rentals	0.006	0.052
184.	Laundries and dry-cleaning	0.015	0.019
185.	Other personal services	0.010	0.022
186.	Advertising, including radio and television	0.019	0.013
187.	Business services	0.004	0.007
188.	Automobile repair services and garages	0.010	0.031
189.	Other repair services	0.006	0.023
190.	Motion pictures and other amusements	0.003	0.013
191.	Medical, dental, and other professional services	0.047	0.010
192.	Nonprofit institutions	0.010	0.013

Productivity, Demand, and Factor Endowments and the Resource Requirements of Trade

Some Preliminary Considerations

In Chapter 3 we used an abstract model in demonstrating how relative changes of productivity, tastes, and factor endowments in different sectors of an economy can affect the resource structure of international trade. We shall use the results indicated by the model in this chapter. Here we wish to examine the relation between the actual changes in productivity, tastes, and factor endowments and the structure of American foreign trade since 1870, in order to see to what extent these three factors can explain the changing composition of trade.

As in preceding chapters, we shall confine ourselves to a long-run aggregative analysis. Using the trade data presented in the earlier chapters plus estimates and information concerning productivity growth, changing tastes, and availability of resources in the American economy and abroad, we shall try to relate the different phenomena in question.

Productivity is at once one of the most controversial and frequently used concepts in theoretical and empirical discussions. Furthermore, the literature concerned with foreign trade often uses it as an explanatory factor. In fact, if we subscribe to the labor theory of value, productivity alone is a sufficient explanation of comparative advantage.[1]

Professor Hicks[2] in his "Inaugural Lecture" relates comparative productivities to balance-of-payments disequilibria and to the international terms of trade. Professor Singer[3] argues that different rates of

[1] See articles by G. D. A. MacDougall, in particular "Some Practical Illustrations and Applications of the Theory of Comparative Costs," *International Social Science Bulletin*, Spring 1951, pp. 59–64.

[2] J. Hicks, "An Inaugural Lecture," *Oxford Economic Papers*, 1953, pp. 117–135.

[3] H. W. Singer, "The Distribution of Gains between Investing and Borrowing Countries," *American Economic Review*, May 1950, pp. 423–435.

growth of productivity in developed and in underdeveloped countries may bring about unequal gains from international trade. An ingenious formula developed by Professor H. G. Johnson relates dynamic balance-of-payments disequilibria to the comparative rates of growth of productivity in the respective trading regions.[4] Finally, we have shown how productivity may affect the resource structure of international trade.

In current economic literature, however, productivity has assumed many different meanings, and only rarely is it used in the sense that we have suggested. Under the name of productivity, we usually find the ratio between total output and a single input. Most often the input will be labor, and "productivity" will correspond to the total physical output divided by the numbers employed or hours worked. This concept is a true index of technological change if only one input is used. Often the concept of productivity refers to capital or, in agriculture, to units of land or livestock.

A number of ambiguities are inherent in the concept of productivity. Productivity measured in terms of any single input may not mean much, for example, in the context of the model in Chapter 3. Consider Figures 8.1a and 8.1b. Both compare two situations of production, A and B, and in both cases labor productivity has increased from 100 at A to 200 at B. Yet, in the first case, no actual change of total productivity occurred; the entire change in labor productivity can be accounted for by the substitution of capital for labor. In the second case, total productivity increased in line with labor productivity from 100 to 200. Only in the case depicted in Figure 8.1b does the model of Chapter 3 apply directly; that is, the production block will expand in the direction of the particular commodity, and all the consequences described there for foreign trade will follow.

But the case of Figure 8.1a is still useful for our empirical reasoning if we deal with it in the setting of the complete foreign trade model. Relative changes in labor productivity in this case still have explanatory value for the changing structure of foreign trade. Suppose that, as in the model in Chapter 3, the economy produces two goods at constant costs (i.e., the two production functions are unit-homogeneous) and uses two factors of production, capital and labor. If increases of labor productivity take the form of a substitution of capital for labor (as in Figure 8.1a), then we can be sure that this happens in both industries, because the capital stock of the economy as a whole is growing.

As a crude first approximation, we can expect that the labor

[4] H. G. Johnson, "Increasing Productivity, Income-Price Trends and the Trade Balance," *Economic Journal*, September 1954, pp. 462–485.

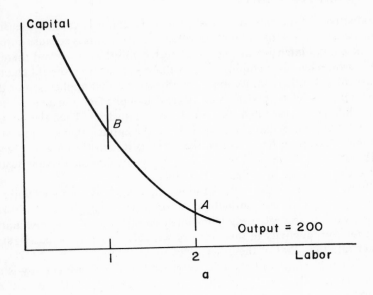

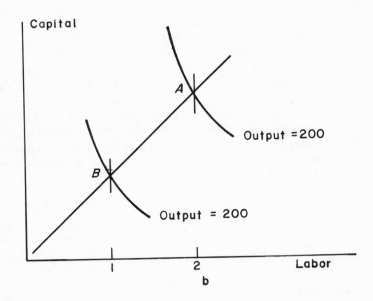

Figure 8.1. Different types of changes in labor productivity.

productivity of the industry whose product is relatively capital-intensive will increase faster than that of the other industry. This is because output of the capital-intensive industry is expected to grow faster and there is no reason why labor employment in the two industries should change drastically. If this is so, we may actually see the first application of the Chapter 3 model, that is, the relative growth of one factor in an economy with different factor intensities for the two industries. Then the impact of faster growth of labor productivity in the capital-intensive industry on the structure of trade will be the same as it is in the case of Figure 8.1b — that is, if the total productivity of the capital-intensive industry is increasing faster than that of the other.

By an opposite argument, it follows that whenever we encounter a faster (or equally fast) growth of labor productivity in the industry which we consider relatively labor-intensive, there is a good likelihood that *total* productivity in this industry has actually been increasing at a faster rate than that of the other industry.

This interpretation of the relative growth of labor productivity is of some interest. It leads to similar inferences concerning the nature of international trade, just as it would if total rather than labor productivities were being considered. Thus, it may furnish part of the explanation why empirical studies[5] often support quite satisfactorily the doctrine of comparative (real) costs.

Another difficulty related to the measurement of total productivity (or of technological change) arises whenever shifts of production functions are not neutral; that is, any time that growing productivity cannot be expressed simply in terms of a scale factor, but is biased toward more use of one factor of production than others.

If innovation is neutral and constant returns to scale are assumed, then the scale factor is a perfectly good index of total productivity. If it is not neutral, the scale factor does not reflect all the information on technological change. Other indexes, reflecting other characteristics of the production function, are needed.[6]

[5] For example, see G. D. A. MacDougall, "Some Practical Illustrations of the Theory of Comparative Costs," *op. cit.*

[6] Assuming a Cobb-Douglas function with two factors of production, a simple estimator of total productivity can be constructed. This estimator can also account for nonneutral types of innovation.

If we take for granted the assumption of a Cobb-Douglas function, an easy check on the neutrality of innovation is provided: namely, the ratio of *money* incomes of the two factors of production must remain constant in time.

It is interesting to note that this check, whatever its value, leads to the conclusion that innovation in the United States over the past 50 years has not been neutral, but capital-saving.

Generally the production function is not known, and only single points of it can be empirically observed. The concepts of scale factor and neutral or biased innovation then lose practical significance, and other means of measuring total productivity are called for.

In the last decade or so, we have witnessed an increasing tendency to combine different productivities of single factors into one indicator of total productivity.[7] This is usually referred to as "total factor productivity." It is designed to reflect changes in productive efficiency only (as does our concept of total productivity) and to leave out the effects of factor substitution. In essence, the idea is very simple and involves the weighting of productivity indexes for each factor into a single index. It is clear that such an index will depend on the weights adopted for combining the individual indexes. In the case of one industry, the weighting problem will be avoided only if factor proportions remain unchanged between the periods compared. But in this case, any individual index of productivity is just as good as the total index. If we deal with an aggregate of several industries (such as mining), the difficulty of weighting is twofold: one problem arises from combining single-factor productivities, the other from combining the aggregated single-factor productivities into an index of total productivity for the sector.

Finally, an important reason for skepticism concerning long-range productivity comparisons is the changing quality of both inputs and outputs. A Model-T is quite different from a 1962 Ford. It is true that volumes of output frequently are derived by deflating value data by a price index. Hence, the number of Model-T Fords is not compared directly with the output of 1962. But this only shifts the difficulty and does not remove it. We cannot escape comparing the price of pears and apples.

Very much the same thing is true of physical factor-inputs. For numbers of workers employed or man-hours the problem may appear less serious, but this is only an illusion. The current procedure is to lump together all types of labor. In this way, however, we risk neglecting changes that have occurred over time in the quality of the labor force. With capital we are bound to run into even more trouble. There is no way of measuring physical changes in the stock of tools, buildings, or

---

[7] See John W. Kendrik, "Productivity Trends, Capital and Labor," *Review of Economics and Statistics*, August 1956, pp. 249–257; G. T. Barton and M. R. Cooper, "The Relation of Agricultural Production to Inputs," *Review of Economics and Statistics*, May 1948, pp. 117–126; and Jacob Schmookler, "The Changing Efficiency of the American Economy, 1869–1938," *Review of Economics and Statistics*, August 1952, pp. 214–231. Estimates computed by some of these authors will be encountered later in this chapter.

raw materials by a single index. We always have to revert to some type of valuation of capital assets, none of which gives a satisfactory answer. What, in fact, we mean when we speak of physical inputs of capital at different periods of time is a puzzle to everyone who has considered this problem seriously.

Attempts have been made to get around the problem of the changing quality of labor by dealing with value inputs at constant prices.[8] The merit of this device is questionable. Here again, deflation of values rather than reckoning of physical inputs only shifts the problem to another plaɲe and does not eliminate the basic difficulty.

We have presented here just a few of the many reasons for exercising caution in using productivity estimates for long-run comparisons. Nevertheless, we must use such estimates, hoping that certain magnitudes derived from statistical observation actually reflect the true state of technology. We may now turn to the data.

United States and Foreign Productivities

In Chapter 5 we made a distinction between crude foodstuffs and raw materials. This breakdown of resource products lends itself well to analysis of the impact of demand. These two groups may be expected to have different income elasticities: The first is subject to Engel's laws; the second is determined as a derived demand of the manufacturing sector of the economy.

Now, however, we are concerned primarily with the conditions of supply of resource products. It would be an oversimplification to deal with coal and cotton in a single aggregate. The supply conditions of these commodities are certainly affected by the different ways in which land enters their productive processes. Consequently, a differentiation between replaceable and nonreplaceable resource products also appears to be necessary.

We take the manufacturing sector as a standard of comparison. Absolute changes of productivity in primary producing sectors cannot tell us anything about the impact of technology on the changing composition of international trade, or on its resource content. We have to compare these changes with changes in the remainder of the economy. Moreover, it will be necessary to obtain information or at least to make some plausible assumptions about similar changes in the rest of the world.

In Figures 8.2, 8.3, and 8.4, and in corresponding tables in the appendix to this chapter, we present some information on changing

[8] See Jacob Schmookler, *op. cit.*

productivity in agriculture, mining, and manufacturing in the United States.[9] For convenience, we use a semilogarithmic scale.[10]

In general, there seems to be a good correspondence between the different series. It may well be, however, that we are not facing an

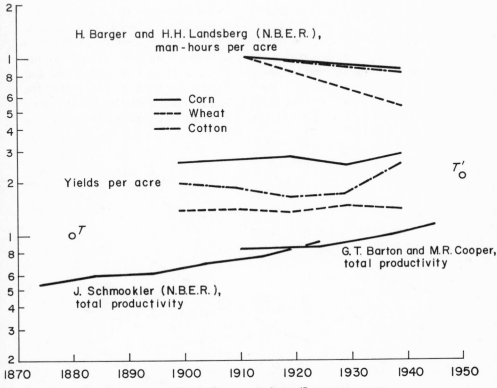

Figure 8.2. Productivity in United States agriculture. (*For sources, see appendix to this chapter.*)

[9] It should be observed that the agricultural sector is narrower than that which we actually should consider, i.e., the "replaceable resource sector," which includes both agriculture and forestry. Note, however, that trade in lumber (the only product of forestry entering our definition of resource products) is negligible relative to that in farm products.

[10] Let us recall at this point that in a semilogarithmic diagram: (1) two overlapping series can be linked together by a simple shift upward or downward of one of the series in such a way that the two series coincide at the chosen linking year; (2) straight-line trends correspond to constant rates of growth; (3) one series can be multiplied by another by adding, and similarly for division; (4) parallel trends mean equal rates of growth; and (5) signs of change (of slopes) are preserved.

[95]

independent sample, since a majority of the estimates come from the workshop of the National Bureau of Economic Research. In certain cases where different rates of growth appear for two overlapping series of different construction, discrepancies can be explained reasonably well.

In Figure 8.2 we find two series of total farm productivity. Schmookler's estimates pertain to entire decades; we have plotted the individual estimates in the middle of the periods considered. Barton's estimates refer to separate years. Both series are constructed as a ratio of the value of total output and the value of all inputs, both taken at constant prices. Roughly the same rates of growth are apparent in the sections of the two series which do not overlap. In the 15 years following 1910, somewhat different rates of growth may be explained by the

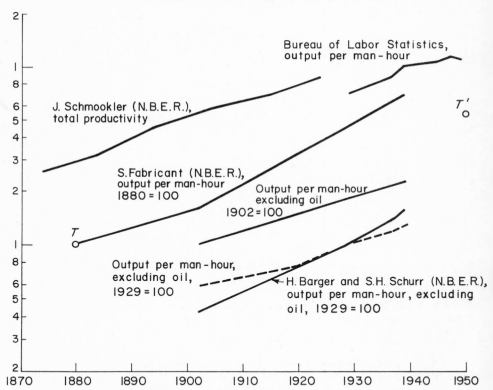

Figure 8.3. Productivity in United States mining industries. (*For sources, see appendix to this chapter.*)

different periods over which estimates were taken. A straight line roughly fitted to the two series would show an annual rate of growth over the entire period of about 1.08 %. We have not drawn in the trend line; but the two extreme points corresponding to such a line are indicated by T and T'.

As a check, and for later reference, we have shown Barger's results for three important crops: corn, wheat, and cotton. Yields per acre as well as man-hours per acre are shown. By subtracting the latter from the former it is possible to see that these results agree fairly well with the trend of total agricultural productivity. The somewhat higher rate of growth of labor productivity which would be obtained in this way could largely be explained by gradual substitution of capital for labor.

Turning to Figure 8.3, we are immediately struck by the higher rates

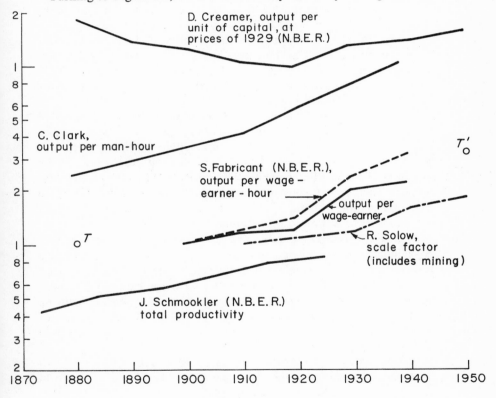

Figure 8.4. Productivity in United States manufacturing. (*For sources, see appendix to this chapter.*)

[97]

of growth of both total and labor productivity in the mining industries. Here we have only one series of total productivity, constructed by Schmookler in the same way as his series for agriculture and manufacturing. As might be expected from important improvements of mining techniques, on the whole this series shows a comparatively lower rate of growth than the others which relate to labor productivity. The comparatively slower growth of labor productivity before 1902 shown by Fabricant, coupled with an inverse pattern of total productivity, reveals the intensive mechanization in mining which did not start until the early decades of this century. From both pairs of series (estimated by Fabricant and Barger, respectively) we can deduce the important contribution of oil production to the rapid growth of labor productivity in mining. The results obtained by the two writers are quite consistent. The only series which reaches into the postwar period is that of the Bureau of Labor Statistics. It definitely shows a slowdown of the rate of growth of labor productivity in recent years. A deceleration of the growth of productivity in the extraction of oil is a component of this change of trend. An imaginary trend-line between points T and T' in which we express growth of total rather than labor productivity shows an annual rate of growth of 2.44 % for the entire period.

Finally, in Figure 8.4 we have recorded six different estimates of productivity in American manufacturing industries. Here again, as for agriculture, we have estimates of total productivity for the entire period: Schmookler's for the earlier decades, and Solow's for the years between 1910 and 1950. The latter are actually estimates of a scale factor of a homogeneous production function whose isoquants are assumed to shift in a neutral fashion. We have encountered this case in Chapter 3 and in the introduction to this chapter.

Both series show comparable rates of growth for the entire period. A slight acceleration may be observed in Solow's series for the last two decades. This is compatible with increasing productivity of both labor and capital during this period. The latter series, prepared by Creamer, is interesting. It shows an increasing capital-labor ratio in manufacturing until about 1918 and a general decrease thereafter. In fact, only in this second period of growing labor productivity can we be sure of actual shifts of isoquants toward the origin.

Both Clark's and Fabricant's results indicate faster rates of growth in American labor productivity in the period beginning with World War I. In both cases, the over-all rate of growth is close to 1.68 % per annum.

Information concerning productivity trends in the rest of the world is meager and considerably less accurate. Not too much can be inferred from Clark's results.[11] Although Clark's treatment of productivity in agriculture is inadequate for drawing conclusions concerning comparative growth of productivity in the United States and abroad, his series concerning productivity per man-hour in manufacturing (for different countries) are more satisfactory. Clark's inquiry covers 15 countries representing well over 90% of the world's manufacturing production.

Only three of his series cover the entire period in which we are interested: the United States, the United Kingdom, and Canada. Canada shows somewhat higher and the United Kingdom somewhat lower rates of growth of labor productivity in manufacturing than does this country. Toward the end of the period, a similar acceleration in the United States trend will be found, as compared with the other two. The bulk of statistics of the remaining countries covers only the period beginning with World War I. While in the decade immediately following the war there might have been a faster increase in productivity due to postwar recovery in the rest of the world as compared with the United States, this relationship is later reversed, until 1940.

An important setback in manufacturing productivity occurred again during World War II in leading manufacturing countries outside the United States. While Clark's figures do not reach into the postwar period, evidence of faster growth in the rest of the world will be obtained from Table 8.1. We again recall the importance of the countries listed

TABLE 8.1

Output per Man-Hour in Manufacturing

	1948	1949	1950	1951	1952	1953	1954	1955
O.E.E.C. countries	87	94	100	106	107	111	116	124
United States	90	94	100	99	101	104	107	112

SOURCE: G. D. A. MacDougall, "Does Productivity Rise Faster in the United States?" *Review of Economics and Statistics*, May 1956, pp. 155–176.

there in the total manufacturing capacity of the free world.

Except for the United Kingdom, all major O.E.E.C. countries have realized a considerably higher rate of productivity growth than has the United States. Admittedly, some of the rapid increase in O.E.E.C.

[11] Colin Clark, *The Conditions of Economic Progress*, second edition (London, Macmillan, 1952), Chapter 6.

countries can be explained again by the postwar recovery, especially on the Continent. Nevertheless, the evidence of recent years indicates that these increases are not temporary.

If we include the two war periods, however, we can conclude with confidence that in the long run United States labor productivity rose faster than that of the rest of the world. But it is not unlikely that in the present decade this general pattern is being reversed.

Even if we take it for granted that productivity in manufacturing was increasing faster in America than abroad, this still would not be sufficient to explain the increasing net exports of manufactures and increasing net imports of primary products here. It might well be that this development was coupled with even more pronounced differential rates of change of productivity in the extractive industries. If we neglect the impact of differences in demand, we can see that net exports of primary products would then increase at the expense of manufactured goods.

In a recent article, G. D. A. MacDougall[12] attempts to give an answer to this problem. Unfortunately, his results are inconclusive, because it seems that none of the estimates for the United States discussed here were familiar to him. In some cases, his results disagree with those we have discussed. But although it is stated in noncommittal fashion, one of MacDougall's conclusions may interest us. His estimates give the impression that during the period between world wars, agricultural productivity outside the United States was rising as fast as it was inside the country, or even a little faster. In the postwar period, however, American farm productivity seems to have increased somewhat faster, at least in relation to the underdeveloped countries. We can conclude that, on the whole, there was a rough similarity between the rates of growth in this country and those in the rest of the world.

We have not found any long-range study of comparative productivities in the mining industries of different countries. It seems also that there are few long-range estimates of mining productivity for individual countries. Yet it can be taken as a commonly accepted view among empiricists that mining productivity has been increasing faster in this country than it has in foreign countries.

Since there are some basic similarities of techniques employed in the extraction of different types of minerals, productivity in coal mining may be taken as a very rough indication of mining efficiency in general. From the table compiled by Colin Clark we obtained the data shown in Table 8.2.

[12] G. D. A. MacDougall, "Does Productivity Rise Faster in the United States?" *loc. cit.*

While in the United States a little over two thirds of the increase falls within the first half of the period considered, productivity in other countries either increased at a rather even rate or manifested more important gains after 1913. A rapid new increase took place in the United States after 1938; the data available suggest that it exceeds the increase in other countries.

TABLE 8.2

Tons of Coal per Man-Shift

	1884	1938
Belgium	0.54	0.74
Czechoslovakia	0.74	1.42
France	0.62	0.82
Ruhr		1.52
Upper Silesia	0.87	1.83
Saar		1.12
Britain	1.18	1.15
United States	1.23	4.37

SOURCE: C. Clark, *The Conditions of Economic Progress, op. cit.*, p. 313.

United States Foreign Trade in Minerals, Replaceable Resource Products, and Manufactured Goods

In Chapter 5, apart from considering the trade in resource products as a whole, we made a distinction between raw materials and crude foodstuffs. Here we want to relate the pattern of trade to changing productivities in different sectors of the economy.

But our former distinction between crude foodstuffs and raw materials does not correspond to any of the currently accepted definitions of productive sectors. For reasons mentioned previously, the empiricist prefers to draw the line between mineral production and agricultural production. It is for these two groups of industries, and for manufacturing, that we have studied comparative productivities. Consequently, we have to divide our trade data into mineral products and renewable resource products.

Originally we intended to estimate the value aggregates for mineral resource products and take them out of Class 1 (raw materials). By adding the residual to Class 2 (crude foodstuffs), we would have obtained total value of renewable resource products. Because we are interested in annual averages for 85 years, this would have required undue effort.

Taking estimates for a few sample years would have distorted the true picture, since important cyclical fluctuations appear in markets of primary products.

Hence, we were forced to adopt a short-cut method — that of taking the total value of principal mineral resource products traded, which also include semi-manufactures. The data required were readily available. As we shall see, this method has many imperfections. Nevertheless, we believe that for the purpose of our analysis it provides the information required.

Actually, the bulk of American foreign trade in mineral resource products is composed of a small number of items: coal, petroleum, copper, crude iron, and steel in exports; and petroleum, copper, tin, lead, zinc, fertilizers, and, recently, iron ore in imports.

Copper, zinc, lead, and tin are imported as both ore and metal, though the refined metal, which enters the class of semi-manufactures, is imported most often. On close examination of import values and quantities of copper, we find that one ton of unextracted copper in ore is only about 20% less expensive than raw (extracted) copper. The 20% differential can be imputed to the value added by processing. Hence, one dollar's worth of copper should contain about 20% fewer natural resources than one dollar's worth of copper ore. But since import prices are stated f.o.b. and transportation of ore is more expensive per unit of its copper content than that of raw copper, the actual difference between the resource content of one dollar's worth of ore and one dollar's worth of raw copper should be even less than 20%. For tin, very much the same thing holds true: The value added by processing is comparatively low. Zinc, which is a rather unimportant item of American foreign trade, manifests a considerably greater difference in resource requirements between ore and metal. This is also true of iron and crude steel. Nevertheless, we feel justified in including iron and steel in our indicator since other mineral resource inputs which enter their production are important.

If we had gone into all the difficulties involved in estimating trade in mineral raw materials for 85 years, we would have registered only the trade of ores and not that of refined metals, whose resource content is highly comparable to that of ore.

We arrive finally at estimates of the values of mineral exports and imports by taking the total value of principal mineral resource products traded. These are: for imports, iron ore and iron, copper and copper ore, tin and tin ore, fertilizers, and the crude-oil equivalent of petroleum and its products; for exports, coal, iron and steel, copper, and the crude-oil equivalent of petroleum and its products. Fertilizers also contain synthetic products, but they are of minor importance only.

These aggregates of dollar value are our indicators of the absolute and relative content of mineral resources in exports and imports. In assessing the value of exports as compared with the value of imports of oil and its products, we tend to overestimate the actual resource requirements of exports. There is, on the average, more value added in exported petroleum products like gasoline and lubricating oil than in imports which are largely composed of crude petroleum or fuel oil. The same seems to be true in general about the character of United States foreign trade in all resource products, especially in more recent years. Hence, our indicators of the relative resource requirements of American trade[13] tend to exaggerate the resource content of exports.

In order now to obtain an indicator of the renewable resource requirements of United States foreign trade, let us return to the two classes described in Chapter 5. Again, we must be content with an approximation. Class 1 (raw materials) is composed partly of replaceable resource products (such as cotton, wool, timber, tobacco, jute, and silk) and partly of mineral products. The second kind of product represents only a very small share of the total value of Class 1 in American exports. This share is more important for imports of raw materials, but except for the most recent years it always remained close to, or below, 20%.

Recalling that Class 2 (crude foodstuffs) is entirely composed of renewable resource products, we can conclude that the bulk of what we have defined as resource products in Chapter 5 (Classes 1 and 2) are actually products derived from renewable resources. Consequently, it is possible, without much distortion, to measure the content of non-mineral resources in American foreign trade by using the results of Chapter 5. The series for mineral resources whose coverage partially overlaps that of Class 2 may provide an additional check (e.g., if our index of mineral resource requirements should show a different over-all rate of change from that of our renewable resource requirements of trade, we could conclude that this difference is likely to be more marked for a "true" index).

The results are shown in Figure 8.5. We have plotted here our estimates of the relative resource requirements (the ratio of resource product

[13] Here let us recall that we mean by the "relative resource requirements" of foreign trade: the ratio of services of natural resources (or resource products) exported to services (or products) imported. "Relative requirements per dollar," on the other hand, compare the requirements per dollar of exports to the requirements per dollar of imports. Clearly, a difference between the relative requirements and relative requirements per dollar will arise whenever exports are different from imports.

exports to resource product imports) for mineral resource products and for renewable resource products (Classes 1 and 2), respectively. Both ratios, that concerning total trade and that concerning trade per dollar, are given. We also show here the actual values of mineral products

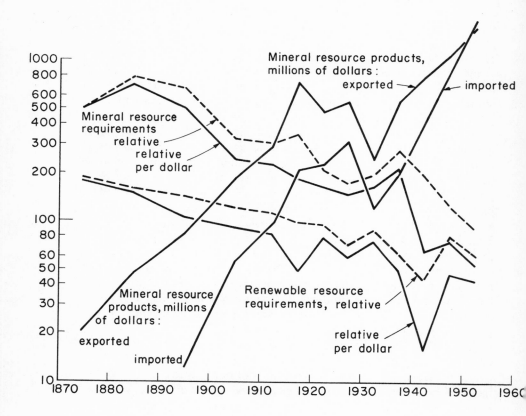

Figure 8.5. Mineral and renewable resource requirements of United States foreign trade. (*For sources and methods, see text and appendix of this chapter.*)

exported and imported, on which the trade-requirement series for mineral resources are based. Similar data for Classes 1 and 2 (our approximation of renewable resource products) were set forth in Chapter 5 and thus are omitted here.

[104]

For the period following 1900, the data presented in Chapter 6 and the entire analysis in Chapter 7 can be used as a check on the two sets of series for mineral and replaceable resource requirements which are shown here. If due allowance is made for the methods of estimation and coverage, we find a satisfactory correspondence between the different sets of data in both cases.

The shares of manufactured goods in international trade are not shown explicitly in our chart, but they are a complement of the resource requirement series. That is, rapidly declining resource requirements of trade imply rapidly growing relative net exports of manufactures. If we include the class of semi-manufactures along with manufactured goods, the series of relative resource requirements of trade and relative trade in manufactures will move in opposite directions and intersect at the level of 100.

Let us concentrate first on the mineral resource requirements. The first observation concerning the 1870's is based on very small values, and hence should not be relied on very strongly. The difference between the relative resource requirements and relative requirements per dollar is again due to a persistent surplus of the commercial balance of trade. The second concept is more suitable for judging the changing mineral resource position of the United States, while the first indicates the value of resources actually paid to foreigners for resources imported.

Both series of mineral resource requirements show a fairly regular decline until World War I. In the period 1915–20, the relative requirements per dollar continued to fall, although in absolute terms the United States was exporting more mineral resources relative to imports than in the preceding five years. A similar effect will be found during World War II. The abnormal high in both series during the late thirties should be imputed to the European armament boom. Following postwar recuperation of a more normal level, a continuing decline can be observed in both series.

A comparison between the two pairs of series clearly indicates a much faster over-all decline in the mineral resource requirements. If we were able to take the mineral resource component out of our indicator for replaceable resources, this difference of trends would be even more marked; that is, the graph of true renewable resource requirements would be flatter than that of Figure 8.5.

Comparing the export and import data on which our relative resource requirements are based, an interesting fact will be observed: Both ratios are decreasing, but for mineral resources the decrease is mainly due to the increasing denominator, while for replaceable resources it is

CHAPTER EIGHT

the decreasing numerator which makes the resource requirements of trade decline. A "normal" expectation would be that both parts of the fraction would be changing in opposite directions in roughly comparable proportions. The asymmetry between our two indicators is a reflection of an expansion of the share of minerals in the total volume of trade (exports and imports taken together) and the decreasing importance of trading in renewable resource products. This, in turn, has two important causes. First, it seems that farmland is a more flexible factor of production than are mineral deposits; it is much more difficult to cope with scarcities of the latter. A whole variety of crops can be grown on the same piece of land, although with different efficiency; but a coal mine will never produce iron ore. The second apparent cause derives from the conditions of demand and changing income. The income elasticity of mineral materials is comparable to that of manufactured goods which use these materials. The latter elasticity is usually expected to be considerably higher than the income elasticity of crude foodstuffs, which represent a predominant portion of the output of renewable resource products in most countries. But even the derived demand for other renewable resource products, such as cotton or wool, may be expected to vary less with changing income than the demand for mineral raw materials.[14] Let us now return, however, to the main topic of this chapter and make our findings more explicit.

Interpretation of the Results

In our model of Chapter 3, we have shown the relation between relative rates of growth of productivity in different sectors of the economy and the structure of international trade. No doubt our model is too simple to explain entirely the variations in our indexes of resource requirements of American foreign trade. Nevertheless, this model can serve as a point of departure.

The rates of change of total productivity found in Figures 8.2, 8.3, and 8.4, through the mechanism of our simple model, would support the behavior of the renewable resource requirements of trade and contradict that of the mineral resource requirements of trade; that is, with all other conditions unchanged (factor endowments, tastes, international terms of trade), and taking into account only the change of productivity, mineral resource requirements of trade should have increased and the renewable resource requirements of trade fallen. Not only did both series actually fall, but also American net demand for

[14] For a statistical illustration, see Table 8.3 on page 110.

[106]

mineral resources has been increasing considerably faster over the past 85 years than that for renewable resource products. Hence, we have to seek the determinants of these changes somewhere outside domestic conditions of efficiency.

The changing relative abundance of natural resources, illustrated by the model in Chapter 3, had a definite influence on our indicators of the structure of United States foreign trade. Population and the stock of reproducible wealth have both increased considerably since 1870.[15] Moreover, these factors of production were increasing at a much faster rate here than abroad. Our abstract model shows the impact of population expansion on the composition of trade. Again, if all other parameters (this time technology and tastes) are neglected, increasing scarcity of natural resources as compared with the rest of the world will bring about trends similar to those of our two resource-requirement series in Figure 8.5.

Thus we have established the expected impact of technology and scarcity of natural resources on the relative resource requirements of American trade. For replaceable resources both effects are empirically verified. In the case of mineral resources, on the other hand, changes of technology would call for increasing relative resource requirements of trade, and the scarcity factor for a decrease of this indicator. Yet the mineral requirements of trade declined at an even faster rate than those of replaceable resource products. Consequently, we have good reason to believe that demand conditions (not yet introduced into our discussion) or some other factor was also responsible for the changes in the mineral resource content of this country's foreign trade. In other words, we have to look for another important reason, or reasons, which would tilt the expected trend of the mineral resource requirements downward while leaving that of replaceable resource products unaffected, or reversing it. Two such factors seem identifiable.

First, it seems that the abstract model of Chapter 3 did not handle the relative scarcity of the land factor adequately. There we dealt with natural resources as a fixed factor of production, while the other productive factors were increasing (one side of the box was expanding, while the other was held constant). This model is adequate as a rough approximation only when we deal with replaceable resource products;

15 R. W. Goldsmith, in his study in *The Growth of Reproducible Wealth of the United States of America from 1905 to 1950*, International Association for Research in Income and Wealth, Income and Wealth Series II (Cambridge, England, Bowes and Bowes, 1952), finds an increase of reproducible wealth of roughly 1000% between 1870 and 1950. Population increased almost four times during the same period.

here, a constant stock of land may be assumed to yield a continuous and constant flow of services. But it is the peculiarity of mineral resources that they are used up in proportion to the service they provide.

In short-run or static analysis we may forget this basic difference between replaceable and mineral resources. But an analysis covering a period of almost 100 years must take it into consideration. Total American oil reserves (present and cumulated past production) were recently estimated at 110 billion barrels;[16] of this amount, well over 40 billion had been extracted by 1957. Although this estimate may be too low,[17] it provides a notion of the orders of magnitude. A similar picture is found for iron and copper ore deposits in the United States. For these two metals, scarcity is mainly a matter of the grade of ore rather than of the absolute amounts of technically recoverable metal. Only a fraction of 1 per cent of iron has been extracted from the total reserves of this country. But it appears that known deposits of high-grade ore (above 60% content) are well on the way to complete exhaustion.

In terms of our model, we can now distinguish three different causes of change in a typical production possibility curve of the United States:

1. The growing supply of non-land resources relative to a fixed supply of natural resources. (This factor is present in both mining and renewable use of resources.)
2. Shrinking base of resources. (This may be imagined as a contraction of the resource-commodity dimension of the production block: it is present in mining only.)
3. Technological change. (This factor expands the production possibility of mining faster than that of manufactured goods and that of the other replaceable-resource sector comparatively slowly.)

Figure 8.6 gives a schematic illustration of these three effects, between 1870 and 1950, for wheat, iron ore, and automobiles.

The remaining determinant of the changing structure of United States foreign trade is demand conditions, or tastes. We are not interested in changes of demand with respect to relative prices; these are endogenous variables of our system, as is the structure of trade which we are trying to understand. It is real income which is the exogenous or predetermined variable here.

---

[16] L. G. Weeks, "Highlights on 1947 Developments of Foreign Petroleum Fields," *Bulletin of the American Association of Petroleum Geologists, 32* (1948), p. 1094.
[17] It has been questioned by the Paley Commission.

1. Growth of non-land factors

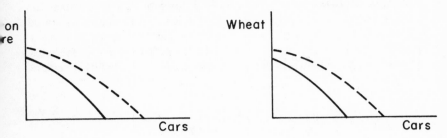

2. Exhaustion of natural resources

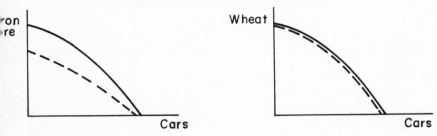

3. Growth of productivity

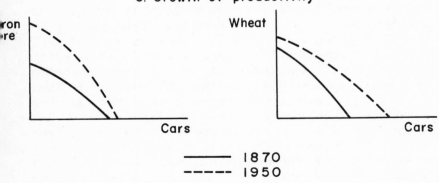

——— 1870
----- 1950

Figure 8.6. Productive capacity with respect to changing nonreplaceable and replaceable resources.

In Table 8.3 we show some of the relevant statistics. The general characteristics of the consumption habits of Americans are apparent from this table. Observe first the satisfactory correspondence between the mining and manufacturing sectors. Real output of the latter increased roughly 22 times, while that of former increased 21 times over 70 years. The difference is very small in view of the crudeness of the estimates. The discrepancy between the increases recorded for the two sectors,

TABLE 8.3

Trends in, United States Agriculture, Mining, Manufacturing, Gross National Product, and Population

Period	Physical Volume of Output (1919–28 = 100)			Gross National Product (1919–28 = 100)	Population (middle of period; in millions)
	Agri-culture	Mining	Manu-facturing		
1869–78	35.0	7.3	10.9	13.4	39.8*
1904–13	85.0	60.0	59.0	64.0	90.7
1938–48	135.0	152.0	238.0	165.0	138.4

* Population of 1870.
SOURCES: S. Kuznets, *Long-Term Changes in the National Income of the United States of America since 1870*, International Association for Research in Income and Wealth, Income and Wealth Series II (Cambridge, England, Bowes and Bowes, 1952), p. 100; *Statistical Abstract of the United States*, 1930, p. 3, and 1952, p. 10.

however, could be explained by increased saving of materials and increased net imports of mineral products. These two factors seem to have been operative in the second half of the period recorded.

On a per capita basis, manufacturing output has increased 530% over the period considered, while agricultural output rose by only 10%. If we deal with income elasticities rather than with physical production per capita, the difference of the two trends is somewhat reduced. These results presuppose an indifference map (as defined in Chapter 3), which favors mineral over agricultural products. (See Figure 8.7.)

Admittedly, empirically established low income elasticities could also arise from asymmetrical changes of the productive possibilities of an economy, even with homogeneous indifference loci. The empirical evidence, however, does not point in this direction. If this had been the case in the United States, the most likely result would have been falling prices of minerals relative to renewable resource products. There is no indication of this happening during the past century.

We are now in a position to add the last factor. While examining the principal features of the long-run supply, we found two factors which supported and one which opposed the important decline in American mineral resource requirements of trade. A moderate decline of the

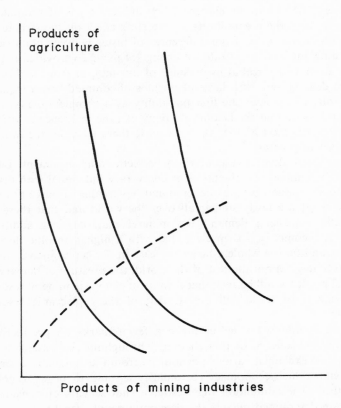

Figure 8.7. Long-range growth of demand for mining and farm products.

renewable resource requirements of trade was found compatible with limited increases in productivity in the farm sector of the American economy. But no satisfactory reason for the more pronounced decline of the first index (mineral resource requirements of trade) seems to follow from the supply conditions prevailing in the different sectors of the American and foreign economies.

It is in demand conditions, then, that the rest of the explanation should be sought. Higher income elasticity of mineral materials as compared with farm products can be found not only in the Unites States but also in other countries. If we assume similar tastes throughout the world, and also similar levels of income, we might conclude that the impact of tastes on the structure of trade was more or less neutral, regardless of the income elasticities of different types of products. In the absence of these conditions, a distorting effect on the structure of trade may come either from differences of tastes between countries or from different levels, and rates of change of income (provided that the tastes are not identical at every stage of income), or from both. Since we are dealing here with large aggregates of commodities, it would be dangerous to consider the first possibility as a complete explanation. We can be sure that the income elasticity of wine in France is different than it is in America; but what reason is there to claim the same for beverages in general?[18]

The second alternative contains a perfectly valid argument. Let us take it for granted that the tastes of an average individual with respect to mineral products on the one hand and replaceable resource products on the other are fairly similar all over the world and that there is a gradually increasing demand for mineral materials per additional dollar of income. It is then clear that with a higher absolute level of income, and on the whole a faster increase in per capita income in the United States than in the rest of the world, the pressure of demand on mineral products will be such that the rate of change in mineral resource requirements of trade will exceed that of the replaceable resource products.

Before summing up, let us make a few remarks on productivity, the principal concern of this chapter. Throughout the foregoing discussion, we explained various phenomena from the behavior of certain parameters which economists customarily assume to be exogenously prescribed. The contention that resource endowments or consumers' tastes are determined outside the economic system can hardly be disputed. The case seems to be somewhat different for productivity. Greater scarcity of mineral resources will probably induce engineers to improve

---

[18] It is sometimes argued that there is some kind of interaction between tastes of a given community and its traditional pattern of production; that is, Americans prefer cars, Italians spaghetti. To what extent the empirical evidence supports this claim is hard to judge. It may be due to different levels of income or factor endowments as much as to different taste patterns. If, however, it were so even for broad groups of commodities, this would only strengthen the present argument.

technology in the mineral industries faster than in other sectors; the mineral industries may be expected to offer more important rewards.

This hypothesis would be a worthless speculation if our statistical evidence did not tend to support it. With faster changes of productivity in the mining sector and the faster-changing structure of trade which we have found, it makes sense to say that mounting scarcity of mineral resources in this country is the dominant factor affecting both technology and the mineral resource requirements of trade, which seem to be complements of each other. Wars tend to curtail foreign availability and stimulate technology; trends are reversed in periods of peace.

Admittedly, technology can cope with resource scarcities in another way, possibly more efficient than that just examined — namely, by substituting abundant materials for scarce materials at the manufacturing level. Aluminum screen windows for copper ones, and nylon stockings for silk, are two good examples. Unfortunately, the tools and information used in this chapter do not lend themselves to the evaluation of the impact of this type of innovation on the structure of trade or on the relative scarcity of natural resources. We have seen in Chapter 5 however, the impact of such *new materials* on the structure of our imports.

Summary

In Chapter 8 we have examined the relation between productivity, tastes, and factor endowments and the resource content of United States foreign trade since 1870. We found significantly different trends of productivity growth among the three principal sectors of the American economy, and between this country and the rest of the world.

Total productivity in mining industries has been growing at a considerably higher average rate than in manufacturing over the past 85 years, while efficiency in agriculture has remained well behind that of the other two sectors.[19] Although evidence concerning the rest of the world is less reliable, we have reason to believe that productivity in manufacturing has grown faster in the United States than abroad. Mining seems to have increased in efficiency faster in this country; no significant divergence of trends is apparent in agriculture.

Furthermore, we find that in the United States the ratio between exported and imported resource products decreased. This trend was especially pronounced for mineral materials.

[19] Indeed, in the most recent period, agricultural productivity has been increasing quite rapidly. This, however, does not change our over-all conclusions with regard to the entire period under investigation.

The evidence concerning relative productivities is entirely compatible with the decline of replaceable resource requirements of trade, but it cannot explain the trend of the mineral resource requirements.

In the case of nonreplaceable resources, we have argued that it is mainly the growing scarcity of mineral resources (relative to all resources, including replaceable natural resources) which offsets the impact of productivity. Another cause of a steeper decline of mineral resource requirements of trade can be seen in the different income elasticities of mineral and non-mineral resource products, combined with a faster growth of the American economy and a higher absolute level of income. A similar asymmetry of spending habits seems to be a key factor in the increased importance of mineral products in total United States international trading compared with other basic commodities.

Statistical Appendix to Chapter 8

TABLE 8.4

Productivity in United States Agriculture

Period	Corn[1] (bushels per acre)	Wheat[1] (bushels per acre)	Cotton[1] (pounds per acre)	Corn[1] (man-hours per acre)	Wheat[1] (man-hours per acre)	Cotton[1] (man-hours per acre)	Total[3] Output per Unit of Input (1935-39 = 100)	Total[2] Output per Unit of Input at 1929 Prices
1945							113	
1937–1940	28.4	14.0	250	85	54	83		
1935–1939							100	
1927–1931	24.7	14.7	171					
1919–1928							85	0.911
1917–1921	27.2	13.4	164					
1909–1918								0.753
1909–1913				100	100	100		
1907–1911	26.5	14.0	186					
1910							84	
1897–1901	25.3	13.8	196					
1899–1908								0.693
1889–1898								0.606
1879–1888								0.587
1869–1878								0.525

SOURCES: [1] H. Barger and H. H. Landsberg, *American Agriculture, 1899–1939* (New York, National Bureau of Economic Research, 1942), pp. 258, 279.
[2] J. Schmookler, *op. cit.*, p. 229.
[3] G. T. Barton and M. R. Cooper, *op. cit.*, p. 123.

[117]

TABLE 8.5

Productivity in United States Mining Industries

Period	Total[1] Mining (1929 = 100) Output per Man-Hour	Total Mining Excluding Gas and Oil (1929 = 100)		Total[2] Mining Output per Unit of Input	Total[3] Mining Output per Man-Hour	Total[3] Mining Excluding Oil Output per Man-Hour
		Output per Man-Hour	Output per Man-Day			
1939	156	128	113		587	222
1937	139	119	105			
1929	100	100	100			
1919–1928				0.872		
1919		74	74			
1909–1918				0.691		
1911			66			
1899–1908				0.568		
1902	43	59	64		158	100
1889–1898				0.457		
1879–1888				0.369		
1880					100	
1869–1875				0.255		

SOURCES: [1] H. Barger and S. H. Schurr, *The Mining Industries, 1899–1939* (New York, National Bureau of Economic Research, 1942), p. 343. [2] J. Schmookler, *op. cit.*, p. 229. [3] S. Fabricant, *Labor Savings in American Industry, 1899–1939*, National Bureau of Economic Research, Occasional Paper 23 (New York, 1941), pp. 45–46.

TABLE 8.6

Productivity in United States Manufacturing Industries

Period	Total[1] Manufacturing Output per Unit of Capital at 1929 Prices	Total[2] Manufacturing Output per Unit of Input at 1929 Prices	Scale[3] Factor A(t)	Output[4] per Man-Hour "International Units"	Total[5] Manufacturing Wage Earner Hours per Unit of Output	Total[5] Manufacturing Wage Earners per Unit of Output
1950	154		180			
1948						
1940			157		312.0	213
1939	135			1.014		
1937			118			
1930	127			0.763	232.0	196
1929						
1919–1928		0.837				
1920			107	0.571	135.0	119
1919	98					
1909–1918		0.765				
1910	103			0.408	117.7	114
1909			100			
1899–1908		0.653				
1900	125			0.343	100.0	100
1899		0.557				
1889–1898						
1890				0.284		
1889	137					
1879–1888		0.507				
1880	183			0.240		
1879						
1869–1878		0.416				

SOURCES: [1] D. Creamer, *Capital and Output Trends in Manufacturing Industries, 1880–1948*, Occasional Paper 41, National Bureau of Economic Research, p. 86.
[2] J. Schmookler, *op. cit.*, p. 229.
[3] R. Solow, unpublished paper on United States technical change (read from a graph).
[4] Colin Clark, *op. cit.*, p. 280.
[5] S. Fabricant, *The Relation between Factory Employment and Output since 1899*, Occasional Paper 4, National Bureau of Economic Research, p. 37.

9

Relative Abundance of Natural Resources in the United States

Introduction

Professor Leontief's two attempts to measure the capital and labor requirements of American exports and imports for 1947 are familiar to all students of international economics.[1] According to these results the United States would appear, contrary to the view generally held, as a capital-poor and labor-abundant country. Leontief and others have suggested that this "unorthodox" conclusion might be challenged by the existence of the third group of factors of production, natural resources.

As an extension of Leontief's investigation, this chapter will study more closely the natural resource content of American foreign trade and use these results to assess the relative abundance of our natural resources.

Much of the theoretical analysis and statistical data pertaining to the subject matter of this chapter was developed earlier in the book. As most relevant, we may recall the general statement of the factor-proportions theory presented in Chapter 4, and the statistics of Chapters 5 and 7. Nevertheless, some repetition is necessary to construct our index of relative resource requirements of United States foreign trade. Clearly, our theoretical apparatus and our data permit an approach to the problem of relative abundance of American natural resources in two different ways: (1) We may crudely evaluate the relative abundance as it has been changing over the 85 years examined, and (2) we may obtain a more precise picture for a single year. The year 1947, for which the Bureau of Labor Statistics structural-flow matrix was constructed, is the best choice.

---

[1] W. W. Leontief, "Domestic Production and Foreign Trade: The American Capital Position Reexamined," *Proceedings of the American Philosophical Society, 97* (September 1955), pp. 332–349; and "Factor Proportions and the Structure of American Trade: Further Theoretical and Empirical Analysis," *Review of Economics and Statistics, 38* (November 1956), pp. 386–407.

In the next section, along with constructing indexes of the *resource product* requirements of American foreign trade, we study the adequacy of these indexes as estimators of the *true* resource requirements of trade. After we present our findings, we use these results in studying critically the relative abundance of natural resources in the United States. Finally, we examine the bearing of our results on Leontief's *scarce-factor paradox*.

The Index of Resource Requirements

Using our definitions, the value of exports and imports in each year can be divided into two components: value of resource products (R), and value of non-resource products (S). It is clear that the resource content of trade would be exactly equal to R only if all resource products were produced by the land factor alone, and all other commodities entering foreign trade were produced by labor and capital alone. In this case, the use of the value of resource products would be a perfect index of the resource requirements of foreign trade. Unfortunately, this is not so. Yet we can obtain reliable information only concerning S and R, and therefore we can observe only the changing shares of S and R over time. From these changes we cannot infer anything about the changing resource requirements of foreign trade unless we are able to make some reasonable assumptions concerning the resource requirements of R and S themselves.

We shall assume that the value of each commodity can be decomposed into two parts: the part imputable to the productive services of land (L), and that imputable to the productive services of other factors (T). Thus we can express the value of resource and non-resource products in terms of these two components. Using the corresponding subscripts,

$$R = L_r + T_r$$

and

$$S = L_s + T_s$$

The index we are interested in is the rate at which productive services of domestic natural resources exchange for productive services of foreign natural resources through American exports (X) and imports (M), namely,

$$I = \frac{L_r^x + L_s^x}{L_r^m + L_s^m} \tag{9.1}$$

The first and crudest approximation of this index, which we may denote by I_1, is the ratio of resource products exported and resource products imported, namely,

$$I_1 = \frac{L_r^x + T_r^x}{L_r^m + T_r^m} \tag{9.2}$$

If we are interested only in the changes of I over time,[2] then I_1 will be the better estimator of I, the smaller the resource content of non-resource products (L_s), and the more stable the share of income of natural resources in resource products (L_r/R) over time.

Let us see how well these two conditions are, or can be expected to be, approximated in the real world.

1. It follows from our definition that natural resources enter the production of non-resource commodities only indirectly, through the inputs of materials which use these resources directly. Consequently, there is a strong presumption that a large aggregate of non-resource commodities will contain considerably less of natural resource inputs than will an aggregate of resource products. Actually, calculations based on the input-output scheme for 1947 (to be presented more extensively under the second approximation, I_2) show that the direct and indirect resource product requirements of resource products exported from the United States were 5.5 times higher than those of non-resource products. A similar computation shows requirements of competitive resource product imports 3.73 times higher than imports of non-resource products.[3] These proportions are not as large as we would like them to be in order to dispose of the L_s terms as negligible. Fortunately, the bias which may result from the omission of these terms in our estimator (I_1) can be expected partially to cancel out between the numerator and the denominator of the index I_1.

2. In order to discuss the second proposition, namely, the stability of the value share of natural resource services entering the aggregate of resource products traded (L_r/R), let us first proceed by an extreme simplification and use the traditional box diagram. This is shown in Figure 9.1. The two dimensions of the box measure the availability of natural resources and the availability of all other factors of

[2] That is, if kI, where k is any arbitrary constant, provides us with all the information we need.

[3] For greater detail and data underlying these results, see Chapter 7 and the appendix to that chapter.

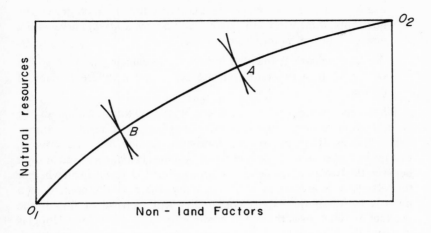

Figure 9.1. Efficient allocation of productive resources.

production to the economy in a given period. From the origin O_1 we measure the inputs of the first commodity (r — or a typical resource product), and similarly from O_2 we measure the inputs of the second commodity (s — or a typical non-resource product). The line connecting O_1 and O_2 is the efficiency locus (contract curve) at which the isoquants of the two outputs touch but do not intersect. Two pairs of isoquants were drawn in the diagram at points A and B. We assume that the two functions are homogeneous of the first order.

The long-run changes in the structure and volume of international trade which we are interested in can be caused basically by three different factors, and can be described by three different changes in our diagram.

a. Domestic or foreign tastes or foreign conditions of output may change. All such long-run changes will affect the terms of trade and leave our box diagram unchanged. Only the equilibrium point of output will move from one point on the contract curve to another. A movement from A to B would correspond to a deterioration in the terms of trade for the resource product.

b. The second possible long-run change in the economic conditions of our simplified economy is the growth of productive resources. This will be reflected in the change of the dimensions of the box. If, as is

[123]

usually the case, it is the capital and labor factor which grows, the horizontal dimension will expand, and a new contract curve with a new equilibrium point will be derived.

c. Finally, technology in either industry may change; most likely this will result in a different contract curve and a different point of production.

What concerns us here is the effect on the relative earnings of the natural resource factor in the export commodity as a result of any of these changes. It is easy to see, granted the homogeneity assumption, that in the first two cases this will depend on the elasticities of subsitution between the two assumed factors of production.[4] Depending on whether this elasticity is greater or less than unity, the resource content of a dollar's worth of the export commodity will increase or fall. If the production function of the export commodity were of the Cobb-Douglas variety,[5] the resource requirements per dollar would remain unchanged, and the resource content of exports would change only with the changing value of exports.

Let us suppose now that technology improves in the export industry. If the innovation is neutral, the same contract curve will apply as before, but its different points will now correspond to different outputs of the export commodity. Consequently, the resource requirements measured in cents per dollar of output at each point of the contract curve will remain the same. The resource content will change only to the extent that the improved technology makes the economy move to another position on the locus. Again, if the production functions were of the Cobb-Douglas type, the resource content of exports would change only with the changing value of exports.

Thus we see that in our simplified model, with unit elasticities of substitution and neutral innovation, our second postulate of unchanged resource requirements per dollar of exports (L_r/R) would be satisfied. For any given product in the real world, however, elasticities of substitution differ from unity, and technology does not advance in a neutral fashion. Consequently, if only one commodity were exported, it would be quite hopeless to make any inferences from the value of exports as to the resource requirements of trade. Fortunately, not one but a large number of resource commodities are traded; and since, as a

[4] That is, the absolute value of the ratio between the percentage change of factor proportions and the percentage change of relative factor prices.

[5] That is, $P = x^k y^{1-k}$, where P stands for physical output, x for the natural resource factor, y for a dose of non-land factors, and where A and $k(\leq 1)$ are constants.

first approximation, we can expect an elasticity of substitution greater than one to be as likely as an elasticity less than one, and innovation to be either land-saving or capital-labor-saving, there is good reason to believe that these deviations will tend to cancel out in a large aggregate of commodities. Thus we may expect that the changes of L_r/R (i.e., of the resource requirements per dollar of exports or imports of resource products) will not be considerable over time.

Although empirical support for this bold contention is difficult to find, it is not altogether lacking. Professor Schultz's estimates show the earnings of land in American agriculture to be virtually unchanged over the past 50 years, at about 25 % of all inputs.[6] Another indication of the stability of income shares of different factors of production in a large aggregate of outputs will be found in the estimates of the aggregate Cobb-Douglas function. Phelps Brown postulates that ". . . there is a considerable agreement among the numerical values of the exponents obtained for different years in one sector. . . . In United States manufacturing, for instance, k was found to lie between .61 and .65 in . . . 1899, 1904, 1909, and 1914; in Australian manufacturing it lay between .49 and .59 in each of four years from 1912 to 1936–37; similarly in Canada."[7] The stability of these coefficients (k) over time precisely implies the stability of relative income shares of the different factors of production involved. This stability cannot be accounted for by the fact that each and every product in an economic sector, such as manufacturing, would have a similar Cobb-Douglas function, and that innovation would be always neutral. But rather we should seek the explanation in the canceling effect of elasticities of substitution higher and lower than unity and in different types of innovation in individual industries.

The above discussion has provided the logical foundation for our first estimator of relative natural resource content of American foreign trade, I_1. The time series of I_1 will be presented and discussed in the next section of this chapter.

Let us now turn to the second estimator of the relative resource content of American foreign trade, I_2. We have observed previously

[6] T. W. Schultz, *The Economic Organization of Agriculture* (New York, McGraw-Hill, 1953), p. 137. Actually the share of "pure land rent" may have declined somewhat. As Professor Schultz points out, the value of farm buildings, which presumably is included in the 25 %, has grown faster than that of land over the period considered.

[7] E. H. Phelps Brown, "The Meaning of the Fitted Cobb-Douglas Function," *Quarterly Journal of Economics,*" *71* (November 1957), pp. 546–650. The coefficient (k) referred to here is the exponent of the Cobb-Douglas production function $P = aL^kC^{1-k}$, where P stands for physical output and L and C for labor and capital inputs, respectively.

that the first postulate concerning I_1 (i.e., the relatively small importance of the resource requirements of non-resource products) does not seem to be satisfactorily fulfilled in reality. We shall make an attempt to account for this in constructing our second estimator, I_2.

Satisfactory information concerning the flows of resource commodities into other industries is not available for the entire period under consideration. Only for 1947 do we have such statistics embodied in the structural-flow matrix of the Bureau of Labor Statistics. These data enable one to compute direct and indirect gross resource product requirements of (1) resource commodities and (2) non-resource commodities entering American exports, and competitive import replacements for 1947.[8]

In order to estimate direct and indirect resource product requirements for the period 1870–1955 from these data, we have made the following assumptions:

1. The resource product content per dollar of resource products remained unchanged over the entire period. This assumption seems quite realistic considering that the gross resource product content of these commodities is predominantly composed of the particular commodities themselves, and hence is never too far from unity.

2. It is impossible to make a similar assumption for the non-resource commodities. Nevertheless, trade in semi-manufactures, by far the most resource-intensive class among non-resource commodities,[9] may be used as an indicator of the resource content of all non-resource products. Thus for each particular period we have estimated the direct and indirect resource product requirements of an average dollar of non-resource commodities exported (or imported) by multiplying the requirements per dollar in 1947 by an index which is related to this year (1947 = 100) and which reflects the relative importance of semi-manufactures in all non-resource exports (or imports).

3. The third and most questionable assumption concerns the problem of competitive and noncompetitive imports. The calculations of direct and indirect resource requirements clearly pertain to the competitive component of American imports only. Moreover,

[8] For the technique and results of such computations see Chapter 7 and the appendix to that chapter.

[9] The reader might find it of interest at this point to consult Figure 9.3, on page 134, where he can find resource product requirements of certain selected commodities on the vertical axis.

even for competitive imports, the direct and indirect requirements of resource products which we can obtain from the input-output computations would reflect the actual factor inputs in other countries only if factor prices and technology were comparable throughout the world.

We do not have any sound basis, however, for evaluating the structural flows of the economies outside the United States, and hence we shall proceed using available statistics. We shall not commit any serious error by imputing the resource product requirements of competitive import replacements of resource commodities to all resource imports. This is because the bulk of resource requirements embodied in a resource product is the particular product itself, whether produced in the United States or elsewhere. On the other hand, imputing resource product requirements of competitive import replacements of non-resource commodities to all non-resource imports requires the very strong and perhaps unrealistic assumption that technologies and resource product prices are similar in this country and abroad. Nevertheless, the bias which may arise from this imputation can be only of minor importance because, traditionally, the bulk of American complementary (noncompetitive) imports has consisted of resource products, while only a negligible part of complementary imports falls into the group of more highly fabricated commodities. Thus the values of direct and indirect resource product imports entering our index tend to reflect the values of competitive replacements together with the values of noncompetitive imports of resource products. In order to make the values of noncompetitive imports of resource products comparable to the competitive imports, we have assumed that the gross resource product requirements (per dollar) of these two components are identical.

Relying on these assumptions, we have computed the second estimator of relative resource requirements of American exports and imports (I_2). It approximates the rate at which domestic resource commodities embodied directly and indirectly in American exports have been exchanged for foreign resource commodities over the past 85 years, assuming that the latter are produced by "average" American technology. Insofar as the second postulate discussed in relation to I_1 holds, I_2 is also an estimator of the rate at which services of domestic natural resources were exchanged for services of foreign resources through United States foreign trade.

[127]

Findings

In Figure 9.2 we have plotted on a semilogarithmic scale the time series of our two estimators of the relative resource requirements of American foreign trade, I_1 and I_2. Both reflect ten-year averages for the period 1870–1910 and five-year averages beginning with 1910. These averages were plotted in the middle of the intervals considered. We have chosen averages over longer periods of time in order to eliminate cyclical fluctuations. Five-year averages were chosen for the later period in order to make the effect of the two world wars more apparent. In computing I_1, we have used data primarily from the *Statistical Abstract of the United States*. Statistical information for the second series was obtained from the same source and from results prepared by Resources for the Future, Inc.

Both series demonstrate similar declining trends; that is, although the United States acted primarily as a net exporter of the services of its natural resources 80 years ago, it has now turned into a net importer of these services. It follows from the construction that the second series, I_2, is a better estimator of the relative resource requirements of American foreign trade. This is due to the fact that I_2 accounts for resources entering trade through resource products, and through non-resource products, as indirect inputs of more highly processed commodities.

The arguments developed earlier suggest that the information contained in the rates of change of our series is more reliable than that contained in their position with respect to the horizontal axis. The vertical location of the two estimators can be assumed to reflect approximately the position of the true statistics only if the resource requirements of an average dollar of exported resource products are comparable to the resource requirements of an average dollar of imported resource products.

Finally, it should be recalled that our two series concern total resource requirements and not requirements per dollar of exports and imports. The series reflecting requirements per dollar would lie below the two series in Figure 9.1 and would demonstrate a somewhat steeper over-all rate of decline. This is due to the permanent and steadily increasing surplus in the commercial balance of this country over the past 85 years.

Changing Resource Supplies in the United States

If our estimators I_1 and I_2 were a good measure of the relative natural resource requirements, that is, if they were very close to the true statistic

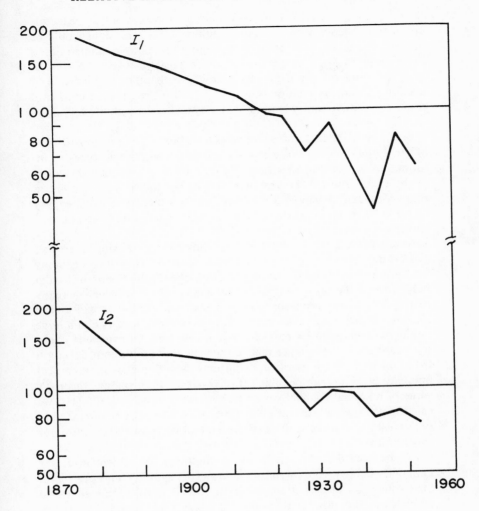

Figure 9.2. Estimators of relative resource requirements of American foreign trade, 1870–1955.

SOURCES: *Statistical Abstract of the United States*, with computations based on the structural-flow matrix of the Bureau of Labor Statistics for 1947. For the method of estimation and interpretation of the series, see the text of this chapter.

I, and if we were living in a world in which the assumptions of the factor-proportions theory were rigorously fulfilled, our conclusions would be quite straightforward. That is, over the past 85 years the United States has become steadily poorer in natural resources relative to the rest of the world and more abundantly endowed with other factors of production. About the time of World War I, or a little later, the natural resources of this country became scarce as compared with the rest of the world.

In reality, things are not as simple as this. First of all, the imperfection of our estimators is of concern. Our indexes contain two types of information of different precision: (1) the direction and rate of change of the trend, and (2) the absolute level of the index at each point in time. Although we can be quite confident with respect to the adequacy of the index as an indication of the direction, we should be cautious in trusting the second type of information.

Another and perhaps more serious difficulty in drawing inferences concerning the relative factor abundance of the American economy is of a more theoretical nature. The Heckscher-Ohlin theorem is valid only if very special assumptions are made, none of which actually corresponds to the conditions of the real world. Moreover, as we have seen in Chapter 4, the existence of three productive factors and a large number of commodities blurs the picture to quite an extent. It is not that we should be willing to defend the view that each minor deviation from theoretically prescribed conditions would make an empirical inference invalid (or impossible). If this were so, the economic theorist's value of marginal product would be very low indeed. But the least we can do is to keep these disparities between the real world and our assumptions clearly in mind and, if possible, learn in what ways they affect our conclusions.

Let us consider the principal assumptions on which Professor Leontief's inferences, as well as our own, depend. We may start with the assumption of zero transportation cost. The revolution in world freight rates took place at about the beginning of our period of reference. Yet, a declining trend in the costs of sea transportation can still be observed down to the end of the past century. Non-zero transportation costs can generally be expected to bias trade against bulky resource products. Increasing efficiency in sea transportation should consequently diminish such bias. Yet, in our context we can hardly go beyond the conclusion that the effect of positive and changing freight rates is on the whole neutral. The bias is likely to operate equally strongly on exports and imports. It might have accentuated the change in relative resource intensities of foreign trade but could hardly have reversed their direction.

We have already observed the persistent surplus in the commercial balance of the United States over the past 85 years. It can be shown that the transfer implied by this surplus should not basically affect the validity of the Heckscher-Ohlin theorem, provided that all its other assumptions are preserved. A transfer will contract the "consumption possibility curve"[10] of one country while boosting that of the other; but the general shape of the production block, depending on the factor endowments, should not be affected.

Unit income elasticity for all goods is possibly the most unrealistic assumption. But it appears that it can be more harmful to Professor Leontief's conclusions than to ours. Yet, even in our case, products defined as resource products may be expected on the whole to have lower income elasticities of demand than the remainder of traded commodities. Note, however, that if income elasticities of resource and other products were equal to unity (all other things being equal), the statistics I_1 and I_2 would be even more markedly declining. In this case, with income increasing faster in this country than abroad, American imports of resource products would most likely not have declined in relative importance after 1920.

Concerning the production functions, it is hard to judge to what extent they actually resemble the conditions of constant costs. We can only be sure of constant costs whenever perfect competition and free entry is guaranteed in an industry and all firms use identical technologies. But decreasing costs are certainly an important driving force in international transactions. They might, of course, explain the gradually increasing specialization of the United States in manufacturing. Whether this could explain the entire decline of our indicator from 180 to almost 70 over the past 85 years is extremely doubtful.

Another important assumption of the Heckscher-Ohlin theorem, not quite independent from the preceding one, is that of equality between technologies (production functions) in the two trading spheres. It is my opinion that these are not identical in the sense defined in Chapter 4. Not only are technologies different from country to country owing to imperfect information, but often in a dynamic world they *are* known in the United States and *not* (or not yet) in the rest of the world. This argument of "new goods" is often used in order to explain chronic dollar shortage and balance-of-payments disequilibria; and it is equally valid for our purpose.

[10] I.e., the production possibility curve minus the physical transfer. Without transfer, the production and consumption possibility loci are identical.

Almost without exception resource products fall within the group of traditional (or "old") goods. "New goods," subject to a strong "demand-pull" exercised in international transactions by the "demonstration effect," are most often of the manufactured variety. This may also be responsible for part of the decline of our indexes.

Natural Resources and the "Scarce-Factor Paradox"

Before concluding this chapter, let us consider briefly the problem of relative factor abundance of the United States vis-à-vis the rest of the world in 1947. We are now in a position to deal with all three factors together and thus to throw some additional light on the analysis by Professor Leontief. In Table 9.1 we have summarized the relevant in-

TABLE 9.1

Domestic Capital, Labor, and Natural Resource Product Requirements per Million Dollars of American Exports and of Competitive Import Replacements, 1947

	Exports	Imports
1. Capital (dollars in 1947 prices)	2,550,780	3,091,339
2. Labor (man-years)	182,313	170,004
3. Natural resource products (dollars in 1947 prices)	340,000	630,000

SOURCES: W. W. Leontief, "Domestic Production and Foreign Trade," *op. cit.*, and our computation in Chapter 7.

formation. Rows 1 and 2 reproduce Leontief's findings concerning capital and labor requirements, while row 3 shows the direct and indirect resource product requirements of American exports and competitive import replacements for 1947.

The latter two statistics are different from Leontief's results in that they reflect values of resource products rather than values (or services) of productive factors. Consequently, the relative resource requirements can be derived from these data only under the assumption that the resource content of an average dollar of exported resource products is at least roughly comparable to the value of resources which would be required to produce an average dollar of resource products substituting for imports. It is virtually impossible to test such a hypothesis. Nevertheless, since very large numbers of different products are traded, we shall assume that it is true. If there is any difference between the resource contents of the two figures in row 3, this difference should show an even more pronounced deficiency of American natural resources. Actually, it is likely that we import commodities containing expensive natural resources and export those containing resources which are relatively abundant in this country.

The information contained in Table 9.1 provides additional support for a known contention,[11] namely, that the factor structure of American exports and competitive imports primarily reflects the relative scarcity of natural resources rather than that of the capital factor. Using the results in Table 9.1, we can calculate the ratios between export and competitive import requirements of capital (C), labor (L), and natural resources (T). Ordering them from the highest to the lowest, they compare as follows:

$$L : C : T = 1.07 : 0.83 : 0.54$$

Assuming the fulfillment of certain conditions of homogeneity and comparability of tastes and technology in this country and abroad, there is a strong presumption that the United States is relatively well endowed with labor, while its natural resources are relatively scarce.[12] Capital, which occupies the intermediate position, is quite difficult to judge. If the natural resource factor could be substituted equally for either labor or capital, we might conclude, although with less assurance, that labor is relatively abundant in this country as compared with capital. This, however, is not the case. While direct and indirect requirements of labor show only very little correlation with the resource content of commodities, we can observe a strong degree of complementarity between capital and natural resource requirements.

The latter proposition is illustrated in Figure 9.3. Along the vertical (logarithmic) scale we measure the direct and indirect natural resource product requirements, while along the horizontal scale we shall find Leontief's capital coefficients. We have selected products of certain sectors according to their importance in American foreign trade and

[11] See M. A. Diab, *The United States Capital Position and the Structure of Its Foreign Trade* (Amsterdam, North-Holland Publishing Co., 1956), Ch. 5 in particular; also, Professor Leontief admits that "clear signs of the influence of natural resources can easily be traced in the capital and labor input figures . . ." ("Domestic Production and Foreign Trade," *op. cit.*, p. 348).

[12] It should be noted that the actual scarcity of natural resources in the United States is probably greater than that reflected by our data. American imports of resource products which do not compete with domestic production are very nearly as important as those which do compete. If the former were included in our computation, at prices which would make them competitive, or even at their actual prices, the third ratio would be well below 0.54.

marked their predominance in exports or competitive imports by (*X*) or (*M*), respectively. The agricultural sector comprises industries 1 through 10 of the classification of the Bureau of Labor Statistics. The resource product requirements of this sector are not those of a consolidated sector, but a simple average of the ten underlying industries. All other points in Figure 9.3 correspond to individual industries.

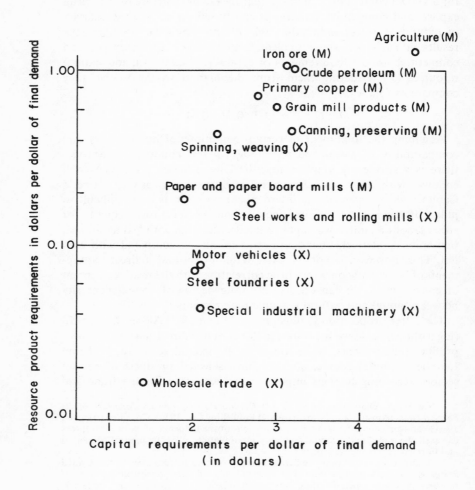

Figure 9.3. Direct and indirect capital and resource product requirements of selected products entering American foreign trade, 1947.

The results in Table 9.1, plus the fact that capital appears strongly complementary to the natural resource factor in the cross section of American industries, lead to an important conclusion. It may well be that capital is actually a relatively abundant factor in the United States. Yet relatively less of its productive services is exported than would be needed for replacing our imports, because resources, which are our scarce factor, can enter productive processes efficiently only in conjunction with large amounts of capital.

10

Conclusions

The primary concern of this study has been twofold. First, we have analyzed the tools of measurement, and the pure theory of the resource content of foreign trade. Second, empirical data were gathered and used in describing and explaining the resource structure of this country's foreign trade. A summary of the more important findings was presented in the first chapter.

Most of this analysis is technical and comparatively narrow in scope. It has an important bearing, however, on a number of broader problems. In several instances, our study either suggests or answers questions concerning these broader considerations. Perhaps the two most important questions that come to mind are the Malthusian dilemma, which postulates the long-range impoverishment of growing populations, and problems of international and national welfare with their related national policies.

There are different ways of measuring the scarcity of natural resources relative to growing world populations. First of all, the common-sense observation may be made that resources, fixed in supply for the world as a whole and any individual territory, are becoming relatively scarcer if total population is growing. Economists, however, usually do not want to define scarcity in this way, and look for some narrower, more economic criterion to answer the question whether resources are scarce. Professor Harold Barnett in a forthcoming study[1] chooses cost relative to an over-all price index as an indicator of resource product scarcity. With the exception of lumber, no significantly growing scarcity was established for the United States in this way. Our export and import unit values of resource products as compared with the general trend suggest on the whole the same thing.

[1] Harold J. Barnett and Chandler Morse, *Scarcity and Growth: The Economics of Natural Resource Availability* (Baltimore, Johns Hopkins Press).

Let us not forget, however, that prices and costs in largely competitive world markets reflect relative scarcities of the world rather than of the United States, whether these statistical indicators are measured in the United States or elsewhere. Thus both Barnett's results and our export and import unit values can indicate, if anything, only the fact that, on the whole, the "apparent scarcity" of natural resources in the world has not changed significantly over the past hundred years or so. Yet, for the United States, natural resources and especially nonrenewable resources have become considerably scarcer relative to other factors of production, as compared with the rest of the world. Our study clearly indicates this fact. What is the same thing, if our country had remained in isolation during the past hundred years and had had no access to foreign markets, at least some resources would have become relatively scarcer according to the cost criterion.

Thus a plausible hypothesis can be formulated that the Malthusian forces actually were operative, but that their impact, in a world where few countries were undergoing industrial expansion, was primarily channeled into a changing resource structure of trade in the growing countries surrounded by a sea of underdevelopment rather than into the expected diminishing productivity. If, say, since 1800 the whole world had developed as this country and the United Kingdom actually did, the reality would have been quite different today. Costs and prices of many resource products would indeed have become higher than the general level of prices.

Consequently, it is only logical to expect that in the future, if all countries succeed in their striving for development, Malthusian forces will have their expected effect, and it will be increasingly difficult for technological innovation and capital formation to offset them.

In the light of these hypotheses, it appears that development of the underdeveloped countries would be detrimental to the well-being of the countries that presently are advanced. It may then be easier to understand why so many are afraid of the so-called population explosion in the underdeveloped countries, and why the actual assistance to the underdeveloped parts of the world is insufficient. Indeed, the higher the population growth in the poor countries, the stronger will be the Malthusian forces affecting all countries by the time the underdeveloped nations reach a reasonable level of industrialization and economic advancement. On the other hand, a high degree of noneconomic altruism can be attributed to those from the developed countries who argue and especially to those who act in favor of the advancement of their economically less fortunate fellow men.

[137]

A closely related problem is that of international distribution of income and welfare in the dynamic process of growth. Ricardo's welfare argument for trade and all its later refinements are static in essence and, in addition to many restrictive assumptions, imply the equality between marginal social and marginal private values. This may be in order for any short-run analysis, but when it comes to long-run considerations, important questions arise. The developed part of the world, almost without exception, is a net importer of large amounts of resource products, while the poor countries are net exporters. If the marginal social and private values and costs were equal, even in the very long run, this situation would be perfectly acceptable. If the social values of resource products, however, exceed the private values generally used in international trading, an important transfer of wealth from poor to rich actually is taking place—just the opposite of what is commanded by Christian ethics, as well as the opposite of what is agreed on internally, by majority decision, in most economically advanced countries of the world.

There are strong reasons to believe that such a discrepancy between private and social values is present. In the time of Ricardo, and throughout the nineteenth century, England was trading under such conditions, and no doubt reaped enormous benefits from its comparative advantage. Where the benefits of its trading partners went is not quite clear. The latter countries, with few exceptions, remained as poor as they had been for thousands of years, or became even poorer.

But the real argument underlying our contention that private valuation of resource products may fall short of social values derives from the fact that private values depend, among other things, on human preferences, which in turn are conditioned by the fairly brief life expectancy of all economic decision-makers. On the other hand, the values of whole nations and societies are based on life horizons far exceeding those of single individuals.

United States transfers to poor countries have amounted in the postwar years to about 0.002 or 0.003 of total national product. In other words, from every dollar of real product of the United States, we give away to nations whose incomes are ten to twenty times lower no more than one third of a penny. Even if we were not willing to accept internationally the kind of welfare transfers we approve within the United States, this contribution appears deplorably small to offset any possible imperfection in the structure of international values.

Index